Hardie Newton's
Celebration
of FLOWERS

Celebration of FLOWERS

Hardie Newton

Photographs by Sunny Reynolds

A Storey Publishing Book

Storey Communications, Inc.
Schoolhouse Road
Pownal, Vermont 05261

Copyright © 1997 by Hardie Newton
Photographs © 1997 by Sunny Reynolds except for:
    Photographs on pages 32, 50, 52-53, 183 (right) © 1997 by Tim Lingo
    Photographs on pages 46 and 144 © 1997 by Hardie Newton

Storey Publishing books are available for special premium and promotional uses and for customized editions. For further information, please call the Custom Publishing Department at 1-800-793-9396.

Library of Congress Cataloging-in-Publication Data

Newton, Hardie.
Celebration of flowers / Hardie Newton : photographs by Sunny Reynolds. — 1st ed.
p. cm.
ISBN 0-88266-997-4 (hc)
1. Flower arrangement. 2. Flowers—Utilization.
3. Flowers—Therapeutic use. I. Title.
SB449.N43 1996
745.92—dc20
96-18918
CIP

Produced by Book Builders/Judd Publishing, Inc.

    Kathleen Hughes, Editorial Director
    Rue Judd, Production Director
    Amy Hammond, Editor
    Kathy Klingaman, Designer

Printed in the United States by R.R. Donnelley
10 9 8 7 6 5 4 3 2

For
My Children
and Teeta

Table of Contents

Foreword

As I sit down and begin to think about what I am going to write for this foreword, I look across my kitchen table and smile. I see the butterscotch-colored morning light pouring over a beautiful crystal vase filled with a circus of brightly colored anemones—and around this vase my two cats are curled up napping.

Suddenly I realize that this lovely scene seems to sum up what this wonderful book is trying to communicate—that true wonder, joy, spirituality, and contentment are experienced most profoundly from the beauty of the natural world and its free and simple delights. These moments of awareness come to us when we slow down, simplify, and bring nature into our daily lives. And as Hardie Newton urges in this book, what better way to practically embrace nature than by planting flowers and gardens and creating gorgeous arrangements for every season of the year.

I had the pleasure of meeting and working with Hardie in 1993 on the American Horticultural Society's National Children's Gardening Symposium and was immediately struck by her natural beauty, elegance, and warmth. She accepted my invitation to present a workshop on flower arranging for children. In she came with armloads of flowers, grasses, and enthusiasm. Soon a crowd gathered around her. Hardie's energy and eagerness to share her love of flowers and flower arranging was irresistible to the children and their parents. The children became engrossed in thoughtful observation of the color, texture, scent, and shapes of the flowers and grasses. Hardie had succeeded in leading these children, as well as everyone around her that day, "into the green."

Growing and arranging flowers is a marvelous and exciting adventure. This book does an excellent job of mixing the inspirational with clear, step-by-step information on the nuts and bolts of flower arranging principles and mechanics. Learning about the simple yet beautiful arrangements that can be made with a number of plants and materials from your house and backyard will show you it is easier than you think to bring flowers into your daily life.

Flowers are so important. They open up special places in our hearts and the hearts of our family and friends, just as this book will hopefully open up places in your heart and mind.

Hardie and Naramata have much to teach you in this book. Read it and allow them to bring you "into the green" where much delight awaits!

Maureen Heffernan
Director of Education
Cleveland Botanical Garden
Cleveland, Ohio

Introduction

Flowers heal our spirits. Whether we are kneeling to plant seeds in the warm spring soil, nurturing the seedlings as they emerge, or arranging the mature flowers in a chosen container, I believe that at their core and ours, flowers speak to us in a unique way.

They feed our souls with subtle energies, providing visual nourishment and irresistible scent. We place them on tables to enhance mealtimes and aid digestion. We eat them, bathe in them, and use them medicinally. They occupy a space on the hall table to welcome the self, as well as the guest. A nosegay by the bed is a last blessing for a good night's rest.

In listening, watching, and surrendering to its joys, the earth will touch us with its rhythms and share the healing secrets of flowers, grasses, weeds, and trees.

Flowers are a way of life. As a language, they and their cousins—vines, shrubs, and trees—awaken our consciousness on an elementary level. I like to think of flowers as the first creative art form, believing they were used by our ancestors to decorate caves and castles.

During the times I take my workshops on the road, away from Naramata, the most beautiful compositions flower spontaneously. Dependent upon a garden club or an arboretum to furnish all the floral materials for a class, I am more often than not surprised by the "ingredients" so generously given, as well as the devoted hours spent in collecting.

One evening before a workshop at the famed Ladew Topiary Gardens, in Harford County, Maryland, my hostess and I lingered over a relaxing after-dinner conversation. Our topics ranged from the next day's timetable to the routine for

A butterfly visits one of the butterfly bushes (Buddleia davidii) in the back garden. At the end of last summer, I noticed a tiny new butterfly bush. It could only have been planted by a bird, because birds and I are the only ones who landscape here at Naramata! This unplanned member of the garden is growing by one of the two arbors behind the house.

setting up the actual workshop. Eventually, we mentioned the all-important flowers, branches, and greens we would use at nine the following morning.

The forsythia, laurel, and pieris japonica had all been cut from the Ladew gardens. Where were the flowers for thirty people? My hostess thought they were at this instant brimming from the windows of my car. I had been assured, or so I thought, that the blossoms for our designs were safely waiting in our work area. Looking at each other dumbfounded, we both caught our breath and then laughed nervously at our predicament. Miscommunication. It happens.

Instead of coffee in bed the following morning, we found ourselves in the midst of colors, shapes, and textures at the flower market. It was six o'clock! The beginning of that day was special. A new friendship had flowered.

Wherever you live—farmhouse or high-rise, city or small town—rejoice in the world of flowers. Celebrate with them, elevate them to stardom. Allow them to touch you. Call them into your life. They graciously give themselves to be used for visual, emotional, and physical nourishment. We thankfully receive and assimilate their essences on both physical and spiritual levels, giving them a place of honor in the living spaces of our homes.

As gardeners, we design living sculptures called gardens and bring flowers indoors to enjoy their scent and color. Common sense tells us that we and flowers have a mutual interest. Aside from beauty, healing, and fragrance, they are basic to our food supply. In planting gardens that hummingbirds, bees, and butterflies patronize regularly, and by caring for forests which manufacture oxygen, we nurture ourselves.

In choosing rugged Virginia land as home, I have learned new meanings and patterns from the changing seasons. Life here brings humorous entertainment, instantaneous insights, unforeseen emergencies, curious people, and fresh inducements to change personal ways of creating.

This book is about being in Nature. It is my way of living. Flowers that grow on this land become more than design elements for lectures or attention-getting arrangements in commercial establishments. Flowers, along with wild things from my woods, are introduced as healing forces. People who already love them and those who are becoming energized by them for the first time welcome their power.

The flowers and other plant materials used in designs for this book are but one representation of numerous possibilities. Given the opportunity, I would, on seeing each photograph, change the compositions completely. Having once solidified a flight of fancy, it is more interesting to see in ever "newer" ways. None of these designs should be considered the "right way;" rather, each is to be thought of as a stepping stone for you, the reader. Take inspiration from them, if you will, going on to be guided by your own heart and intuition. Allow your style to change and develop, remembering that both gardening and flower design are works in progress. They facilitate ever-emerging creative energies.

Writing this book has taken precedence over many garden chores dear to my heart, and I rejoice at the opportunity to return to earth! Truths, taught to me by the spirit of this book, go with me. The path is an endless one in which enrichment grows as a ground cover to protect our feet as we walk.

— Hardie Newton
January, 1997

TOUCH THE EARTH

In the cold of a January morning, I awakened to a
booming voice that said, "I am going to sell this house
and move to the country!" Though I knew full well the voice
was my own, I sat bolt upright in bed, peering into the darkness for some oracle to verify the words.

In that instant, there was a distinct pronouncement that
the time for major change had come. My flower design business and I would move from the metropolitan Washington,
D.C. area to a place of beauty, joy, and solitude in the Virginia
countryside.

Having no idea exactly where I would go or, in fact, what
such a move would entail, seemed no obstacle whatsoever. I
had forever dreamed of countrysides crossed by streambeds
located in mountainous terrain with towering shade trees and
open meadows.

Friends argued that I would be lonely, but their fears were
my desire. Being alone was not a consideration. I was already
alone.

A Move to the Blue Ridge Mountains

By week's end, I was traveling the hundred miles from
Washington to Madison County, Virginia. It was waiting for
me—the land on which I would build a new life.

The estate agent and I stood in fields adjacent to a grav-
eled country road. A winter landscape described the bones of
the land, while imagination outlined gardens that would surround a house of light.

The architecture would be not unlike the plantation house
my father lived in as a boy. Walking through the snow and up

Springtime's redbud and poplar

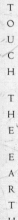
The round baler will be the next actor on the meadow stage of newly mown hay. As soon as the flower heads of the grasses rattle to the touch, they will be rolled into thousand-pound bales of hay to be stored as winter feed. Being a part of the valley's rhythm allows your spirit to surrender to its joys.

a hill to the place where the woodland and meadow met, I could see over the narrow valley to Old Rag Mountain. "Old Rag," as it is called, is a favorite climb for hikers from near and far. The view was twofold: simultaneously rugged and all embracing. These contradictions in Nature felt hospitable. A vigorous lifestyle in inviting surroundings would be both challenging and nourishing.

The agent argued that the land was not for sale. After all, we had stopped on this particular rural road because she was a bit lost and had hoped somehow to find our whereabouts. Being found has never been high on my list of priorities.

Surprisingly, this land was indeed for sale. The process of design began. Twice, I thought I had made the right connection with an architect, with the expectation that forthcoming house plans would match my intentions; twice I was mistaken.

The builder, a man who had lived his entire life in Madison County, and I spoke the same language, so we began without an architect. Over the months it took to make my new home a reality, we worked from blue chalk marks drawn on the sub-flooring, not from traditional drawings. Those were floor plans in the most basic sense of the words.

During this process, my heart held the promise this place would fulfill. People would come here to feel and experience the vital connection to earth, tantamount to our being.

With the house completed, I named the land "Naramata," a Native American word meaning, loosely translated, "The Smile of the Great Spirit."

The Rhythm of the Valley

Miles from my former environment, settling into the way of life that is Naramata seemed effortless. I observed the path of the sun as the seasons changed, fell asleep to the sound of a fox calling to her kits, gardened under a moon so full that its light shone from the trowel gripped in my hand. My senses opened to these singular surroundings. I felt where I lived.

Walking the upper streambed one spring Sunday in search of wild orchids, I looked for hours, finding none. A neighbor assured me they were there. My eyes had hunted diligently, but at the wrong height. The flower I sought was only six inches tall. There was a multitude of showy orchids (*Orchis spectabilis*), natives of Virginia, celebrating spring's arrival by welcoming me into the neighborhood. Learning to see is not always effortless.

Soon after moving to Naramata, I invited new acquaintances to come for dinner. They lived nearby, which in the country can mean fifteen minutes away by car. As late afternoon became dusky evening, we sat on the porch noticing cars and trucks that traveled up our country road, along with fireflies that began their evening dance. Plumes of dust stirred up by the passing trucks were followed later by headlights that marked each vehicle's journey, looking like giant fireflies.

Later, as the guests were leaving, one smiled and said to me, "Hardie, I'll bet you develop a good relationship with that road of yours." I have. On a still night, it is easy to identify the trucks by the sound of their engines. Over the years, the road has become one of the melodies of time. I can gauge the day— or season—by sounds in the valley. The winter school bus tells me it is either seven fifteen in the morning or four fifteen in the afternoon.

The voices of the birds sing of dawn or dusk. The deer have a distinguishable call in the dark. This place allows me to be in tune with the earth from the moment I wake until the time to sleep again under a moon whose light makes patterns across the bed.

Surrounded by foothills that adjoin Virginia's Blue Ridge Mountains, my house is actually built into one of those

foothills. From its verandas, I look down on the convergence of five streams that have helped to form the valley floor. From the double front doors, I walk straight uphill over rocks, through streams, and around fallen trees to circle boulders covered with lichen. Passing through a grove of ancient mountain laurel near the top, it is evident that this is a popular haven for deer.

Twenty-Nine Doors

During the early months, the promise of Naramata was a constant companion. The promised dream continues to unfold.

Naramata invites all who come here to join in a relationship with Nature. It is a place of safekeeping where people meet the land, allowing it to facilitate the awakening of their potential.

The house has twenty-nine glass doors—and no windows—all of which open onto wide, covered porches. From these porches, restful vistas of valley or forested hillside bring a sense of peace to both guests and students. The feeling of stability given our human root system at such a moment is not forgotten. A world is there to emulate. We see textures and shapes to be mirrored in new imaginings. Naramata is a place for those who wish to become a part of the basic composition of wild earth: its grasses, flowers, weeds, shrubs, trees, and outcroppings of rock. To these gifts from the land, each student brings a fresh interpretation: his or her own relationship to flowers.

The many glass doors of the house afford a constant communication with its wooded environment. I can almost touch the blue mountains in the distance, watch the ladybugs awakening in the spring, inhale the fragrance of the forest, and taste the rain-filled clouds overhead on a humid summer night. Being a part of the valley's rhythm allows my spirit to surrender to its joys. Collecting moss-covered logs, fallen birds' nests, and selected rocks to accompany flowers and herbs from the garden in tablescapes and in impromptu flower arrangements is only a part of my life here.

Denim and Pearls

There is comfort in contrasts. I hike these foothills in boots, denim, and pearls, and work the gardens with bare hands, feeling the soil drink away moisture from my skin. Walking the land strengthens the body. Carrying bags of composted manure and bales of straw is reminiscent of gymnastic workouts in the city.

At the end of the day there are the rocking chairs, good books, and contemplation of new projects. "Work" takes me into conference centers, country inns, and restaurants to design large arrangements of fresh flowers—many of which are cut from gardens of the particular establishment. "Work" also invites me, as a lecturer, to speak to fascinating groups of people. Although I speak on flower design, I always return home filled with stimulating ideas given freely—gifts from my "students."

Touch the Earth

I have always needed to touch the earth, to live close to it and allow its nourishment to fill me, from childhood days of gardening alongside my mother to life today, gardening and working with others as they challenge their creative abilities through the medium of flowers.

It is my conviction that, if we are able, we return to the haunts of childhood.

I grew up on a mountaintop in Tennessee, surrounded by woods, searching for arrowheads, playing hide-and-seek among magnificent, four-foot-tall zinnias and golden marigolds in my mother's garden. The landscape of my childhood included a chicken yard, a whole grove of rhododendrons, and a tiny stream where my young hands worked at landscaping from the

As you can see, I am a "denim and pearls" type gardener.

age of five. Life was organic then. What wasn't eaten from the summer garden was canned for winter. Strawberries placed in flat, glass-covered platters were baked in the sun and called strawberry preserves. Fertilizer was real manure.

Lavish tea parties were just the thing for favorite dolls who sat in little chairs circling a rock formation filled with rain-water. The spring parties were crowned with violets plucked from the edges of the woods. In the summertime, the dolls "ate" vegetables still warm from Mother's garden.

Later, life as a married woman was dictated by the structure of my husband's profession, and our family moved every few years. Continuity came from digging a new garden at each successive home. The fact that these gardens never reached maturity under my hand had no real relevance. Pleasure came from the actual process of planting, encouraging life to spring from the earth as I watched. This same sequence was repeated in dozens of gardens, hundreds of miles apart. I did not wear denim or hiking boots in those days.

My husband and I often gave parties, filled with interesting people. The greatest pleasure of these gatherings, for me, was planning and arranging the flowers. Using materials native to particular geographical areas reflected the beauty of that day's environment. Sometimes, there were huge assortments of flowers on a grand piano. On other occasions, a fragrant rose in a nondescript container gave a sense of quiet elegance to an evening with friends.

Whether minimal or grand, my adult flower designs tell the truths I have known since giving those first childhood tea parties. My essence is nourished through relationship with the natural energies and healing qualities of our earth. Its flowers, weeds, trees, rocks, water, and mountains are the messengers.

Herbal and Floral Remedies

Years went by, and in my fifties I began a new era, that of a single woman. My attention turned to learning new ways with flowers: the study of holistic healing. Herbal and homeopathic remedies were a natural outgrowth of this interest. Simultaneously, my diet changed and I began meditating. A more disciplined mind began to comprehend the essence of tranquility.

I have come to understand that by galvanizing my own energy forces through proper nutrition and the practice of meditation, my creative self is more liberated and lighthearted.

Sometimes when ambling through the woods, I am attracted to what could be called a "fairy ring." This circle of trees of one variety seems magical to me—a circle of energy. If silent in

I used blue veronica (Veronica spicata 'Blue Peter'), pink larkspur (Consolida ambigua), Queen Anne's lace (Daucus carota), and pink floribunda roses (Rosa 'The Fairy') to decorate a children's tea table. The vase was filled to the top with water at seven in the morning and thirsty occupants drank an inch of it within a two-hour span. Cut flowers drink the most water during the first twenty-four hours.

*Drawn porch shades in their protective midsummer mode. I added rosemary (*Rosemary officinalis*),* French *lavender (*Lavendula vera*),* geraniums *(*Pelargonium*), and a jade tree to counter the verticals of the porch railings. The three porches, integral parts of the day-to-day Naramata activities, serve as transitional spaces between the in and out of doors.*

such spaces, my spirit becomes infused with that selfsame energy. A sense of wellness ensues. Wisdom repeatedly tells me I am living in a protected place—a land called Naramata.

Flowering

As the house neared completion, I began planning for classes and workshops. Each participant would need ample area in which to work; thus, both tabletops and individual pedestals would be required. Using the porches as workspace was part of the original plan, as it places individuals in immediate proximity to their environment.

Beginning each workshop with a short demonstration, I stress techniques that help prolong the beauty of the forthcoming arrangements. This includes mechanics, tools, and conditioning, all of which we will discuss here. Participants—be they men, women, children, or entire families—begin to shift gears, get the feel of the land and visibly relax. As we plan our day together, we touch on subjects of intuition and feeling and discuss our gifts from the earth. The emphasis is on our inherent ability to learn from Nature on all levels.

Soon, it is time to gear up for a walk in the woods. We include picnic lunches, buckets in which to carry found materials—rocks, lichen, gnarled roots—and walking sticks.

Our uphill climb from the red front doors is along a streambed that flows down from a collection of moss-covered rocks surrounded by ferns, roots, and shade-loving wildflowers. Clambering upward, pausing to swing on an ancient low-hanging grapevine, we slowly become a part of the rhythm of the forest.

As we near the rocky outcropping that is a perfect spot for lunch, the group has quieted and begun to notice the immediate surroundings: wildflowers, wild mushrooms, old mossy logs, weathered roots, lichen-covered rocks, and vines growing high in the trees. After lunch, everyone fills his or her bucket with a few special objects, making sure not to take things that cannot be quickly and naturally replenished.

Back at the house, each person creates in an individual workspace. Sounds of laughter, suggestions, and comments fill the air. Throwing out old notions of what an arrangement "should" look like and the "rules" that "must" be followed, these flower-lovers begin to seriously create. Everyone shares flowers, materials, encouragement, compliments, and critiques. There is astonishment at the variety of designs. Students sweep things onto drop cloths as they work and, during cleanup at the end of each workshop, there is a perceptible change in each.

Those who have never arranged before, and some who arrive at Naramata literally trembling in anticipation of failure, find new, relaxed attitudes by listening to their own inner voices while selecting, combining, and creating in ways that bring satisfaction. It is wonderful to be with others during a first experience of "letting the flowers do the arranging." Usually sorry to leave, they have a sense of personal accomplishment and contentment that shows in smiling faces. The flowers have done their work.

The promise of Naramata came true for me during a morning design workshop one year after moving here. The house was filled with people diligently working at individual pedestals. I went outside to gather more branches and greens and, coming back to the house with full arms, I stopped in my tracks.

The front doors were wide open and, looking in, I saw each person concentrating quietly on his or her own design. The fragrance of the flowers, the birdsong, the sound of the nearby stream said it all. A process had been set in motion; each would now go on in an inspired way, taking home from Naramata a basic joy: the feeling of being a partner in Nature.

Your Turn to Flower

In the chapters ahead, we will discuss arrangements that can be artless or elegant. The imaginative designer in each person can allot dream time for incorporating flowers, fruits, vegetables, rocks, and logs into ultimate intrinsic beauty. We will be creating four different seasonal arrangements in the identical roll-neck terra-cotta pot. (A papier-mâché florist's liner is used to ensure that the arrangement is leakproof.)

When beginning any flower arranging project, having a few "tools of the trade" at hand facilitates spontaneity.

- clippers or knife
- heavy-duty pruners for large branches
- papier-mâché or plastic liner, if your container needs water-proofing
- container of choice
- floral foam
- preservatives
- dry foam
- poultry wire
- floral wire
- chenille wires
- davey tape
- floral tape
- clear tape
- hyacinth sticks or bamboo garden stakes
- water tubes

Branches, flowers, and greens

Freedom

Tools of the Trade

Pictured below are the tools you need: Row 1 (bottom row, left to right): edges trimmed from papier-mâché liner to fit into the terra-cotta pot; chenille wires; clear florist's tape; spool wire; wire cutters; water tube; pocket-sized clippers; small glass vase.

Row 2 (left to right): terra-cotta pot and saucer, fitted with papier-mâché liner and filled with two vertical blocks of floral foam, secured by davey tape; floral tape; dry foam for dried or silk flowers; cylindrical vase topped with clear floral tape, applied in a grid fashion; single blade knife; six-inch tall glass vase; papier-mâché container filled with poultry wire.

Row 3 (left to right): glass vase with davey tape mechanics in grid pattern across top; ginger jar-shaped glass vase with poultry wire taped over opening; heavy-duty clippers for pruning

shrubs and cutting woody stems; standard floral foam block.

Row 4 (top row, left to right): floral tape; ginger jar-shaped glass vase holding green hyacinth sticks; davey tape; floral tape.

Basic Tools

Clippers or knife. Whether you prefer clippers or a knife to prepare your flowers, it is essential that the tool have sharp edges. Dull blades tend to mash stems, blocking water absorption. My preference is a medium-sized Swiss Army knife. In my opinion, a knife gives a cleaner cut, allowing the flower to drink water more efficiently. Stems cut on the angle provide a greater surface for water absorption.

Heavy-duty pruners. Invest in a good pair of pruners, as well as a sharpener. They will last a lifetime. There are both regular pruners and ratchet-style ones to choose from in the catalogs or at garden centers.

Containers and Liners

The container for your arrangement can be anything appealing that you already have on hand, one that fits the overall tone and visual parameters of a location: a water glass, terra-cotta saucer, basket, crystal vase, grandmother's punch bowl, or a copper bucket. The question to ask yourself is, "What am I trying to accomplish?" Using the most simple, unadorned container emphasizes the character of the flowers. On the other hand, unpretentious spring blossoms can set off a superb antique vase, while a charming art object containing a few flowering branches shows both to great advantage. The point is, you always have options: emphasize the flowers, the container, or give equal value to each.

Liners, for use in metal containers with questionably welded seams, in flowerpots with drainage holes, or in leaky antique porcelains, are sensible alternatives to ruined tabletops. Liners can be anything from a florist's papier-mâché container to a plastic butter crock or glass bowl. The main concern here is to reliably waterproof your creative efforts.

Floral Mechanics

Water, no mechanics. It is not always necessary to use floral foam, wire, or tape to secure flower designs. When you have a narrow-necked vase (e.g., water glass or crystal vase) and perishable flowers, an arrangement can be made by placing flowers directly into a vase filled to the top with water. By interweaving their stems as you go, the flowers support one another. We'll

The most important angle in basic flower mechanics

learn more about this method in a later chapter. Just remember, when you use clear vases, you must change the water regularly, and it is easier when there are no rigid forms holding the flowers. Cloudiness in the water indicates bacterial growth, which begins to develop after three or four days—signaling that it's time to empty the vase. To facilitate the change, lift the entire bunch of flowers out of the vase (their stems will be interlaced). Lay the bunch on a table or counter and wash the vase with hot, soapy water. Place the empty vase on its side, reinsert all of the flowers, then refill the vase with water and preservative. Always keep the water level as near the top of the vase as possible. Flowers drink the most water within the first twenty-four hours of arranging.

Floral foam. To anchor an arrangement like our seasonal ones, we use two blocks of floral foam cut to fit the liner. Floral foam, which is used for fresh flower material and can be found in any flower shop, hobby shop, or nursery, is available in several weights: springtime, instant, deluxe, standard, and large designer blocks. Standard is the grade recommended for overall use, as it is sturdy and soaks well. Place the floral foam in a deep container of water for at least one hour, and preferably overnight, giving it ample time to drink up the needed water. Fit the soaked floral foam snugly into the papier-mâché liner or into the container itself.

If the container or liner is deep and rather narrow, turn the floral foam on end, rather than stacking the blocks one on top of another. This ensures proper "wicking," that is, continued absorption of water added to the finished arrangement over the coming days. The floral foam should be at least two inches higher than the lip of the container to accommodate downward-sloping vines, branches, or flowers.

Preservatives. My favorite preservative is ordinary bleach, mixing one tablespoon to a gallon of water. Commercial floral preservatives are also available in powder or liquid form. Your own preference is the one to follow here. Bleach solution can be used in metal containers; packaged ones available from your florist cannot be used in metal of any sort.

Dry Foam. Dry foam, like floral foam, comes in the shape of a brick and is brown. It is specially made for dried plant material or silk flowers and does not absorb water. The texture is similar to styrofoam.

Poultry wire. Poultry wire is helpful, mechanically speaking, in three ways. First, to act as a steadying technique for narrow-necked vases, cut only a small amount of wire to size, fitting it over the actual opening of the container. Secure the wire to the top of the vase in three places (using davey tape cut into strips two inches long.) Note the photograph of tools in this chapter as you work.

Secondly, if you prefer to use only water and preservative in a container, poultry wire is the alternative method for holding flower stems securely. In this case, form the wire into a ball (or whatever shape fits your vase) and fit it loosely into the required space.

Third, poultry wire is used as an added support for floral foam if extra-large-stemmed flowers or branches are a part of the design. Cut a piece large enough to fit over your foam comfortably and secure the wire to the sides of your container with davey tape, as mentioned above.

Floral wire. Wire can be purchased as spool wire for constructing wreaths, or in several lengths. Both types are available in various weights: #18, #21, and so on. The weight indicates the size of the wire and is chosen according to the job to be done.

Chenille wires. Chenille wires are wires covered with chenille (similar to pipe cleaners), inserted into hollow-stemmed flowers, such as daffodils, for strengthening.

Davey tape. Making sure your flowers stay put in the face of any eventuality is crucial. Place davey tape in a grid pattern over floral foam, securely attaching it to the sides of your liner or container. If the arrangement is to be moved about, an additional piece of tape circling the container, overlapping the original strips, gives maximum security. Davey tape is a heavy-duty dark green cloth tape with adhesive on one side. One roll will last for dozens of arrangements and can be purchased by the roll also as "split tape." The split one affords a narrower tape for use in smaller scale designs.

Floral tape. Floral tape comes in two shades of green, white, dark brown and some pastels. It is lightweight, has a waxlike finish, and is useful for making bouquets. It sticks to itself, but to nothing else!

Clear tape. Clear tape has an adhesive backing like Scotch tape and comes in rolls. It is used to section off the top of narrow-necked vases in a grid pattern. It holds and balances stems, decreasing frustration during the beginning stages of work. (Davey tape can also be used in this same manner.) Arranging without mechanics is a learned technique developed with practice over time, and clear tape is a stepping-stone toward that goal. It is preferable to davey tape when used with glass, because it is invisible.

Hyacinth sticks or bamboo garden stakes. Hyacinth sticks can be purchased in several sizes. I prefer the fifteen-inch length, finding it generally more serviceable. It, of course, can be cut shorter if needed or lengthened by attaching another stick to it with davey tape.

Bamboo stakes, which can be bought from your garden center, can be taped to water tubes and used for lengthening flower stems.

Water tubes. Water tubes are plastic tubes with rubber tops that are particularly helpful if a flower stem needs to be elongated. They come in many sizes and are easy to attach, using davey tape, to a long hyacinth stick or bamboo garden stake. They are especially helpful in the case of a broken flower stem.

Branches, Flowers, and Greens

Branches. Well-shaped woody material (shrubs and trees), branches in bud, and full-flowering branches are all appropriate and readily available. Branches add height, texture, color, and dimension to an arrangement. As you would expect, stripping away all the leaves from a branch gives more impact to the blossoms. You might choose to strip off the blossoms and keep just

Pictured here are my outdoor gardening tools and soil enrichers.

the leaves. Third, keeping both blossoms and leaves to a minimum and utilizing barer branches adds drama and line.

You can begin to use woody material indoors to nourish your flower and sun-starved soul in late winter. Here in Virginia, I have forced forsythia *(Forsythia)* in the latter part of January by placing it in deep, warm water in a bright place of sixty-five or more degrees.

Your sources for spring blossoms are almost endless. Ask your neighbors for branches trimmed from their ornamental trees, and keep on the lookout for farmers who are pruning their orchards in late winter. I have loaded apple cuttings into my car, then left them on a cold porch for a month or more before bringing them inside to force. Apple blossoms in early March are a great harbinger of spring.

If you live in the city, you can find interesting material as you walk your dog (or just yourself). Choose well-landscaped streets for your walks! With ready clippers in your pocket, and certainly with permission from the homeowner, you will help them prune branches that are hanging out over sidewalks. You and your dog will have had a happier walk, and attractive linear material will be the honored dinner guest. In January, February, and March you will begin to find ornamental branches, pussy willow *(Salix discolor),* and forsythia in flower shops.

Preparing branches for your arrangement is quite easy. Slender branches should be given a sharp, diagonal cut across their base. Before an overnight soak in warm water, the stems of larger woody material should be slit two inches from the base and the outside bark shaved off to a depth of three inches. Alternatively, to allow them to drink up water efficiently, the stem ends may be crushed with a hammer (especially lilac branches). To make sure larger branches are firmly footed when using floral foam, square off their sides with a knife before inserting them in the foam. Rounded stems have the tendency to twist about or wobble, particularly if they are oversized.

If you are forcing blossoms, allow two to four weeks for the buds to open. Branches cut further along into spring will have fatter buds, and the forcing time will naturally decrease. Humidity is a crucial ingredient in flower development indoors, and daily misting is one way to provide needed moisture. You may also encase the branches in plastic bags for a greenhouse effect. Either way, when the buds are quite swollen, a move to a sunny window will give more color to the opening flowers. Experimenting is the only way to determine the real length of time needed in your own environment for forcing all branches.

Suggested woody materials for flower arranging include the following:

most fruit and flowering trees
aucuba (*Aucuba*)
azalea (*Rhododendron*)
boxwood (*Buxus*)
butterfly bush (*Buddleia*)
camellia (*Camellia*)
elaeagnus (*Elaeagnus*)
euonymus (*Euonymus*)
flowering cherry (*Prunus*)
forsythia (*Forsythia*)
hydrangea (*Hydrangea*)
Japanese maple (*Acer palmatum*)
magnolia (*Magnolia*)
mountain laurel (*Kalmia latifolia*)
nandina (*Nandina domestica*)
photinia (*Photinia*)
pine (*Pinus*)
pussy willow (*Salix discolor*)
quince (*Chaenomeles*)
redbud (*Cercis*)
rhododendron (*Rhododendron*)
rose (*Rosa*)
spirea (*Spiraea*)
viburnum (*Viburnum*)
weigela (*Weigela*)
witch hazel (*Hamamelis*)

Flowers and greens. There is hardly a flower, flowering shrub, or piece of greenery that can't be used in your arrangements. As any gardener knows, arranging what you have grown is doubly satisfying. Perennial borders, cottage gardens, and cutting gardens are all wonderful sources for seasonal flowers. If you are not a gardener, don't be shy about asking friends for leftovers. Many gardeners grow in such abundance that they are happy to share their wealth.

Don't forget potted plants. If your gardening space is limited to a sunny windowsill or apartment balcony, you still have a source for flowers and greens. House plants to keep on hand for your arrangements are azaleas, begonias, cyclamen, ferns, ficus, geranium, hibiscus, ivy, palms, kalanchoes, and other succulents.

The bounty from a vegetable garden can be used as a still life by adding only a few flowers. A great way to get children to enjoy their summer vegetables is to let them eat the center-piece! These are more delectable, of course, if just picked from the garden or purchased from the farmers' market.

Wildflowers are striking additions for your work, and it's tempting to denude a country roadside to fill a flower basket. The thoughtful, careful gatherer avoids cutting to excess in areas where other passersby will also enjoy the natural beauty. As with flowering trees, in many states it is illegal to cut flowers along public roadways and in parks; and it is unlawful ever to pick some plants. Even if you know people who welcome you to their fields and meadows to gather, show respect for the land while you walk on the wild side. Remember, next year's crop is dependent on this year's seeds for reproduction.

Flowers that emerge from bulbs and tubers for inclusion in your list are amaryllis, anenome, calla lily, crocosmia, daffodil, dahlia, eremurus, freesia, gladiolus, iris, hybrid lily, ranunculus,, tuberose, and tulip. Caladium —also a bulb—has insignificant flowers, however the leaves add impact to arrangements.

Autumn's rich colors: an arrangement which "emerged" from a fall workshop

Other sources are the commercial florist or supermarket. When you need to budget, try visiting your florist on Friday afternoon as they are cleaning out their cooler for the weekend. You may be able to negotiate lower prices.

Flowers cut in full sun will usually wilt and droop quickly. If that is the only time of the day you are able to cut your flowers, plan on arrangements lasting no more than twenty-four hours. In this instance, avoiding floral foam and placing flowers directly into a vase of warm water gives greater longevity. We know that the heat of the sun brings out fragrance in herbs and flowers by day, and there are biologists who tell us that the life force of all plants returns to the root system while they, too, are at rest during the night. It makes perfect sense, then, that in early morning, flowers are just beginning their cycle of rejuvenation (circadian rhythm). Remember that butterflies need the heat of the sun for flying. Think how we feel when the sun warms our backs. Consider that flowers "become" as well. We want to pick them when they are at the pinnacle of their own beauty, thus brimming with life force. When cutting garden flowers, I prefer the hours after sunset.

Conditioning flowers before arranging them is basic. Cut the stems of garden or store-bought flowers on an angle with your knife or sharp clipper; remove all dead leaves and greens that will be below the water level and immediately plunge the stems into deep, warm water, preferably in a nonmetal container. The right temperature will feel just like milk from a baby bottle tested on the inside of your wrist! Putting them in a cool, dark place allows the flowers to soak up lukewarm water overnight. To help ensure maximum vitality and water absorption, I take my plastic bucket of warm water to the garden when cutting. Consider the fact that it is an enormous shock for a flower to be cut in the first place. Caring for them and giving them the gift of quiet recuperation can be considered in another way as their meditation time prior to a public debut.

Remember that cool temperatures add longevity to flowering life, while warm temperatures promote exquisitely full blossoms. There are probably as many tricks to keeping arranged flowers fresh as there are flower arrangers, so listen carefully to what your friends recommend and take notes! One method is to mist them with a water-filled spray bottle on a daily basis. Others feel that cutting stems under water will make flowers—especially roses—last longer.

Roses can be revived by cutting the stem anew, wrapping the flower heads in newspaper for protection and standing the

Queen Anne's lace adores blooming and is a "long laster" in water or floral foam. Consistently shedding on tabletops, it seems fragile and is airy and cooling in summer's heat. Find it everywhere!

stems in almost-boiling water for several minutes. Other drooping flowers, such as candytuft (*Iberis*), dahlias (*Dahlia*), salvia (*Salvia*), snapdragons (*Antirrhinum*), and sunflowers (*Helianthus*), respond to this very hot water method, as well. Before reusing containers and buckets, make sure they are scrubbed thoroughly with soap and hot water to prevent bacterial growth.

Freedom. Believe that you, your imagination, and your freedom of spirit are the most important ingredients for this ephemeral work of art, a creation of flowers. Spontaneity and willingness to experiment are two qualities that will guarantee pleasure and satisfaction. When all of these come into play, rules will be easy to use, when applicable, as you listen to what the flowers wish to say. You and your intuition create artistic flower compositions as a team. Flower arranging is one of the highest of art forms, producing beauty, fragrance, and healing—for the arranger and for all comers as well.

Chapter 6 includes a glossary of flowers, shrubs, and trees for flower arranging. Check there for seasonal suggestions, including as many as possible in your landscaping plans.

Helpful Hints

Here are quick hints to get you started...
1. Cut flowers after sunset, if possible.
2. Cut stems of flowers and greens on an angle to provide a larger surface for water absorption.
3. Cutting flower stems underwater—especially roses—prevents air bubbles from traveling up the stems. It is not necessary with all flowers, so do experiment.
4. To condition flowers for arrangements, place cut flowers and other materials in a plastic bucket (never metal) filled with deep, warm water. When conditioning euphorbia, however, put the flowers in their own bucket of cool water; otherwise the florets tend to mildew.
5. Cut peonies when almost full-blown. Ants are the "opening agents" for peonies. Bringing peonies indoors means bringing ants indoors.
6. Tender spring growth wilts easily (examples: magnolia, ivy).
7. To determine the freshness of roses, press them tenderly at their base. They should be firm to the touch.
8. Remove only the thorns below water level when conditioning roses. Thorns to a rose are like fingernails to a human.
9. Remove "guard petals" (the outside ones) of florist roses, before arranging them.

My grandson Christopher, age nine, concentrates on his masterpiece. Children lose themselves in the world of flowers, so intently absorbed that they are startled if someone speaks to them. Christopher and I have "played" together with flowers for three summers now. When he visits, we habitually collect part of our lunch from the fields: cress (Barbarea), violets (Viola odorata), violet leaves, and poke (Phytolaca americana) for our salad greens. (Note: Poke becomes poisonous after it is more than 12 inches tall.)

His flowers, which we also gathered together, are spider flower (Cleome hasslerana), goldenrod (Solidago odora), phlox (Phlox paniculata), cosmos (Cosmos bipinnatus), black-eyed Susans (Rudbeckia hirta), and zebra grass (Miscanthus sinensis zebrinus).

10. Examine the underside of bought flowers to determine their freshness.
11. Have a plastic bucket of warm water at your side when cutting from the garden so that you can put materials and flowers directly into the water.
12. Enjoy the abundance of each flower "in season."
13. Invest in a good, heavy-duty pair of pruners for cutting woody branches.
14. Split ends of woody branches before conditioning. Hammer the cut ends of lilac branches.
15. Burn the cut ends of poinsettias and euphorbia until they quit sizzling to add longevity to the blossoms, even when they are to be placed in water.
16. Keep knives and clippers very sharp. Clean cuts prevent the mashing of stems.

17. Flowers maintain their stamina longer in fresh water (with preservative) than when placed in floral foam. Preservatives include ordinary bleach and commercial products available from your florist.

18. "Standard" grade floral foam is the best type for general use.

19. Change the water in glass containers every two to four days, also adding fresh preservative.

20. Cut flowers drink the most water in the first twenty-four hours.

21. Keep all containers full of water, no matter what mechanics are used. If you do so when using floral foam, the stems will be less inclined to become clogged with foam.

22. Remove all foliage (leaves) below water level to prevent bacterial growth.

23. In planning arrangements, consider using flowers of similar longevity.

24. Avoid removing, then reinserting flowers in the foam. The block disintegrates easily once full of holes.

25. Cut off spent flowers in bouquets, rather than pulling them out. Cutting does not disturb the remaining flowers. Replace with fresh flowers.

26. Use davey tape for stabilizing floral foam in containers.

27. Use davey tape, clear floral tape, or poultry wire across the tops of glass vases to hold flowers in place.

28. Davey tape dislikes water. Keep the roll in a dry place.

29. Use a number twenty-two or twenty-four wire to wire stems of flowers (roses, gerberas, tulips). Wires come in different lengths and weights (meaning sizes); the lower the number, the heavier the wire.

30. Use spool wire (available also in "weights") for assembling wreaths and garlands.

31. Floral tape is the answer for taping flowers together into bouquets. It is useful also for covering wires, as in a "taped wire." Twist the tape tightly around the wire, starting from the top of the wire. Use one hand to turn the wire, while the other hand holds the tape. (This is a difficult thing to learn!)

32. "Taped wire" helps to hold unruly flowers or branches in place. (For example: Secure a taped wire to the handle of a basket, then twist it around a recalcitrant branch or piece of unmanageable grape vine.)

33. Bamboo stakes or hyacinth sticks to which water tubes have been attached should be used to lengthen short or broken flower stems.

34. Remove stamen from lilies; their pollen will stain clothing.

35. Hay, straw, dried leaves, collected mosses, rocks, and lichen are great disguisers for floral foam.

36. The tops of curly willow branches (available from the florist) inserted in a glass vase act as "frogs" for stabilizing flower stems.

37. Grow interesting flowering plants indoors for use in designs.

38. Forced-air heat pulls moisture out of flowers. If possible, keep flowers away from heat outlets, air intake vents, and fans.

39. During collecting trips to gather materials such as mosses, lichen, stones, or weathered roots, leave the area as undisturbed as possible.

40. Cut wildflowers sparingly, remembering that Nature needs to reseed every year.

41. Collect only bird's nests that have fallen or have been abandoned in the winter.

42. Hornets' nests are safe to cut down after the first frost.

43. I was taught by an old Native American woman that all rocks need rainwater. Keep collections out of doors to maintain their health.

Goldenrod (Solidago odoro),
yellow-orange alstromoeria
(Alstromoeria), *orange celosia*
(Celosia argentea), *chrysanthemums*
(Chrysanthemum *'Garnet King'*),
variegated pittisporum
(Pittosporum undulatum),
solid aster (Aster novi-belgii),
and swamp grass.

Pam Kirkland, a student of several years, created this fanciful dance of alstromoeria which crowns a deeper-hued mix of fall flowers: 'Garnet King' chrysanthemums, purple asters, orange celosia and goldenrod. Swamp grass and variegated pittosporum are the greens.

44. To eat well, grow your own vegetables and fruits.

45. If you want to feel healthy, work with flower energy on all levels, eat appreciatively, and exercise joyfully!

46. Be alert to regional flowers, new ideas, and unusual containers during your travels.

47. Prune evergreens in the winter when they are needed for holiday arranging.

48. Water tubes may also be used in a reverse manner. Insert dried material into "dry" water tubes for consolidation with fresh flower arrangements. This keeps the dried material from absorbing water from wet floral foam.

49. Observe Nature carefully, making an effort to imitate natural proportions you see in the wild. Soon, you will design instinctively. Let imagination guide your waking dreams.

*The garden
when I was a little girl
I had
forever.*
— *Anne Edwards (nine years old)*

SPRING

Where there is life, there is spring. Violets appear in country lanes and beside city sidewalks. Being conscious of our surroundings, we hear Nature's voice as it speaks to us saying, "Look at the flowers; witness birds, bees, and butterflies at their work!"

As spring begins to flourish, a repeated rhythm of Nature becomes gradually more apparent. All of our senses respond to the warmth of the sun, beauty of the earth, and fragrance of the flowers. We awaken, crawling out from under the rock of winter in harmony with the rest of earth's creatures. Chief Seattle reminds us that "the wind is sweetened by the meadow flowers."

In spring, the heart becomes lighter, more inspired—just looking at daffodils blanketing a hillside or a park overflowing with cherry trees feeds the soul while the body begins its spring healing and feels more alive. Bloodroot beckons from the edge of the woods. We go to sit in the forest and contemplate the emergence of these earliest flowers. A crescendo of robins' wings calls our gaze upward to witness sudden flight. Landing on lawns and in meadows, the same robins speak of the unseeable as they pull worms from under young grass.

For those in the city, there are relaxing weekend picnics with walks in favorite parks and neighborhoods. Florist shops brim with primroses. People move with a different energy. Their instincts—if obeyed—carry them into garden shops to hunt for seeds they forgot to order from last winter's catalogs. Roaming through gardens, large or small, they begin to rake winter's leaves from tiny, pale green shoots. Apartment dwellers change the soil in planters, envisioning new miniature landscapes to brighten their balconies or windowsills.

Japanese pittosporum (Pittosporum tobira 'Variegata'), French tulips (Tulipa 'Flame'), snapdragons (Antirrhinum)

Earth-colored pottery is an excellent choice to add to your collection of containers. It can be a primary accent or act as a grounding artifice for flyaway tulips and snapdragons. I placed variegated pittosporum in the vase first as a foundation for the flame tulips and the expressive yellow snapdragons, which were added in groups. Because I wanted the flowers to "speak up," I left them to condition in their bucket of water for twenty-four hours, near a window, so they could become shapely. Tulips continue to grow after they are cut and eternally reach towards the light, giving their stems individuality. If you wish them to "stay put," as would be true in a symmetrical centerpiece, draw the draperies and shut the room's doors to keep out the light until time for your dinner party. Kept in the dark, their manners are impeccable!

had drenched my jeans, invaded pockets, and covered my boots with mud, grass seed, and straw.

Such moments are mysterious and reverential. When I started this job—still looking like a normal person—there had been eight pounds of grass seed, four bales of straw, and great patches of mud. Now, the bags and bales were only a memory, and everything had taken on a new form, including me. I learned that it takes two hours to spread four bales of straw, but only forty-five minutes to broadcast eight pounds of seed and the same amount of time to cover boots with mud, add a layer of seed, and touch them up with a generous top-dressing of straw.

More importantly, the memory of those moments will fill far more hours than the actual time I spent in the field that spring afternoon. Despite driving rains, the straw held, and the grass seed soon transformed the muddy field into a beautifully green meadow.

Ladybugs and Violets, Robins and Bloodroot

In very early spring the ritual of holly berries and robins proclaims spring. Entire air wings of red-breasted birds descend upon twenty-five-foot holly trees, which are heavy laden with plump, red berries. The robins sing and gorge themselves until they are too sated to fly. After spending several hours banqueting, they retire to nearby trees to recuperate, now quiet, ready to nap away the afternoon. Spring binge, I call it. It's just Nature's way of emptying the trees for the tiny white flowers to come—fragrant bee attractors, which appear in June to begin the cycle anew.

Whether in the country or city, early spring brings the first glimpses of forsythia *(Forsythia x intermedia)*. The vibrance of its energy-giving chromium yellow is an instant tonic. Indoor forcing of forsythia branches can produce blooms as early as January and is a wonderful preamble to the coming of spring. Wherever you are, find a forsythia bush and clip a few budded branches to place in a container of deep, warm water. Situated in bright light, the blossoms will soon open. The waiting and watching process is a nurturing one. A birthing in miniature takes place before your eyes.

Here in Virginia, there is synchronization between the appearance of forsythia in the garden and small bloodroot blossoms *(Sanguinaria canadensis)* poking out from under winter's dead leaves and fallen branches. Overnight, hundreds of these multi-petaled white blossoms carpet the forest floor. Flowers come first, looking rather like small yellow-centered, creamy water lilies. The foliage follows, little green hands pretending to

An armload of pink and white dogwood brings an instant canopy of color into my front hall.

be leaves. If a child is visiting, I often dig the soil away from one of these little flowering plants to explore the source of such an odd name: a long root containing red juice that gives the plant its old names, bloodwort or "Red Indian paint." The root, used herbally, is a blood cleanser—but poisonous if taken in too great a dosage.

Even if unconvinced by the bloodroot, robins, and forsythia, the arrival of spring is indisputable when the edges of Naramata's woods begin to color. The redbuds *(Cercis)*, timidly at first, begin to announce their presence; soon their brilliance is astonishing. They are followed by a burst of dogwood blooms (*Cornus florida*) that send waves of pink and white through the forest. Each fall at Naramata, I dig saplings of these two trees and transplant them from their hiding places deeper in my woods to the forest perimeters. They get more light and grow faster there. The ultimate goal is a wide border of spring color framed by elegant verticals of maples and beeches. My horticulturist son has taught me that the younger a tree is when transplanted, the faster it will settle into its new surroundings.

Spring also announces its arrival inside as the house turns into a "ladybug hatchery." For several years now, hundreds of ladybugs have spent winter hibernation with me. Every winter afternoon as the clock strikes two and the westering sunlight warms the glass doors, they stretch their legs and come out of the tight little communes formed in the uppermost and darkest reaches of the guest room. Walking through that area while they are exploring can be hazardous—for the ladybugs, that is— especially if we human occupants are wearing hiking boots, as I generally do. A game of ladybug hopscotch ensues as I try to avoid stepping on those crawling about the floor. I have watched to see if they graze on insects harbored by the house-plants, but they seem to be just happy sightseers, until suddenly their inner clock tells them it is human tea time, the hour they usually retreat to a secure corner.

My ladybug housemates greet the spring equinox with her-aldry and fanfare. At precisely seven o'clock on April twenty-first, they awake. Flying into my hair, walking on my collar, scal-ing the walls, moving from mostly self-imposed confinement in one room from which only the adventurous had strayed earlier, they cover the entire house. When the doors to the porches are opened, the flight to freedom begins.

Sometimes, as I urge the tiniest "ladies" onto bits of paper for transport outside, I wonder if my friends have, indeed, been breeding and not just hibernating over the winter. Helping them make a debut into the natural world riding on paper chariots is now an anticipated spring ritual.

Like ladybugs, violets (*Viola odorata*) are an enduring sign of spring and have a generosity similar to bloodroot: they appear quite abruptly and in great profusion. Somehow, violets always find children. Has there ever been a child who could resist pick-ing a bunch for Mother or a friend? The next time you give in to the irresistible urge to pick violets on a spring day, eat a few as you walk along (as long as you know that no pesticide or herbicide has been applied). They seem to lighten up all those

Overleaf: Candy tuft (Iberis) *and* dogwood (Cornus florida) *provide a framework for a wild and distant aged pear tree.*

interior spaces of the body that have grown stagnant during winter quiescence. With the flowering of forsythia, bloodroot, and wild violets, the earth's period of rest and rejuvenation is over.

Profusions of hybridized jonquils (*Narcissus jonquilla*), like tulips (*Tulipa*), give us several weeks of bloom, extending the season with spring's nourishing colors.

When the tulip (*Magnolia kobus*) and star magnolia (*M. stellata*) trees bloom in the garden, I make haste to promptly enjoy their beauty. Both, being sensitive to frost, are invariably nipped if the weather turns chilly once again. These trees have elegance during the winter, too, since at that time their branches are covered with charming furry catkins, unusual in shape. They dry well, placed in a container, not especially needing water.

New Gardens

Beginning the gardens at Naramata, it was evident that I knew nothing of soil or weather conditions in this part of the Blue Ridge foothills and that everything was going into the ground on a strictly trial basis. Clove pinks (*Dianthus caryophyllus*) leaped with joy at their opportunity to grow in a new location, while veronica (*Veronica*) halfheartedly produced their spiky offerings in an effort not to disappoint me.

Actually, when planting smaller bushes and perennials, experience teaches that the placement should be considered conditional. After a year in one area, most perennials will tell you that either they are gloriously content in their surroundings or they would like to move a little this way or that. The satisfaction of paying attention teaches a new language: "flower talk."

During the spring that house-building began, an experienced gardener friend volunteered to help transplant perennials from my previous garden. As we worked on the hillside next to the driveway and discussed plans for the new garden, she urged me to consider the planting of fragrant seasonal shrubs and flowers near both front and back doors. With a promise of twenty-nine doors to come, that was a daunting suggestion!

Viburnum carlesii, situated at the double front doors, is one result of her guidance. Its spring fragrance is an instant welcome to Naramata. The heavy scents of a pink lily (*Lilium* 'Le Reve') and white Casa Blanca lilies (*Lilium* 'Casa Blanca') soon follow the viburnum's sweetness, while those indefatigable clove pinks shout their fragrance from the hillside above.

Adding a touch of richness, *Iris reticulata* are one of the earliest garden bulbs to bloom, their royal purple aglow in hesitant late afternoon sunlight. Snowdrops (*Galanthus*) nod as you come unexpectedly upon a group of them at the corner of the house, followed by a large gathering of favorite miniature jonquils, *Narcissus* 'Tete A Tete'.

Creeping phlox *(Phlox nivalis)* was planted on Naramata's hillsides to echo the deep color of the redbud blossom overhead. A dual purpose is fulfilled in that the root systems provide great stability, preventing soil erosion. Throughout their blooming season, little patches of this phlox can be dug to use for disguising the floral foam that anchors a container design of redbud or dogwood branches.

In mid-May, fields and parks in the countryside turn yellow with wild buttercups *(Ranunculus)* and ragwort *(Senecio)*, followed by oxeye daisies *(Chrysanthemum leucanthemum)*, and poppies *(Papaver commutatum)*. Trees and fences, heavy with roses toward the end of the month, promise a crop of rose hips to harvest for winter tea parties.

Unsettling to a person who had wormless soil six years ago, half a worm turning up in the bowl of a busy trowel gives pause. This spring, as an Easter gift to my land, I dug in a few dozen lily of the valley *(Convallaria)* pips, and found a healthy worm population, multiplying satisfactorily. In themselves, they are a joy to behold. All gardeners welcome them. The presence of worms means that the soil is enriched by their castings and is becoming more friable due to their hyperactivity. When I overhear a discussion about digging worms to go fishing, there is a mental alert stating, "Not on my land, you won't."

Angelique tulips frame the potting shed and Virginia's Blue Ridge.

I instantly cover accidentally turned-up worms with a blanket of mulch. Since they wear no sunscreen, it seems wise to protect their sensitivity to surface elements. Perhaps they don't need the extra nurturing, but it heals my sense of guilt at intruding into their daily routine.

Utilizing one well that supplies three gallons of water a minute, I soon realized that this treasured asset was not sufficient to share. From the beginning, it was necessary to use serious mulch in all the garden beds—with a promise to each newly-added garden friend that it would be thoroughly watered-in on arrival, lovingly mulched, and given additional moisture as needed for several weeks. After that time, it would be expected to survive with the rainwater furnished by Nature. I watch with amazement as the gardens flourish, noting that the mulched earth seems to hold moisture evenly and well.

On planting the vegetable beds, I began adding straw (six to eight inches deep) between the rows of beans, lettuces, snap peas, okra, and zucchini. It attracts the dew, holds moisture in

Garden peonies, delphinium, hosta, daylily foliage, ribbon grass, and columbine combine with wild cow parsnip cut from the stream bed.

Grape hyacinths (Muscari armeniscum), *Italian pittosporum, broom* (Genista)

Two paper cups fit the inside of my old six-inch English flower pot perfectly, making it waterproof. Into them I situated small groups of grape hyacinths, careful to cut the stems to varying lengths held together by a loosely fitting rubberband around their base. Sprigs of variegated Italian pittosporum positioned beside the grape hyacinths add textural contrast as well as animation. I cut some of the pittosporum sprigs, available from florists, shorter than others. A few pinches of graceful white broom carry the eye upward, giving a feeling of airiness and informality to the arrangement. Because this design is seen from all sides, the broom is centered. Note: grape hyacinths tend, like tulips, to grow after they have been cut and they fall gracefully over the pot edges in places.

Ranunculus (R. asiaticus),
Bupleurum (griffithii)

*Compactly arranged, peach and pink
ranunculus speak of spring, their colors
sharpened by longer stems of yellow tinged
bupleurum. Many of the well trimmed
stems, because they do not reach the bottom
of the clear glass vase, give a sprightly
sense of the season. Bupleurum, an import
from Holland, adds graceful height to the
more weighty ranunculus heads.*

the soil and discourages weeds. Now it is a mainstay, as again, the vegetables are given no water other than when the seeds are in their germinating stage. Straw can have the opposite effect as well. During very wet times, it can hold too much moisture for some annuals and vegetables, causing mildew and root rot.

HINT — After using half a bale of straw, retie the two holding pieces of twine around the unused part. This cuts down on water absorption when the bales are left outside and makes them easier to lift when moving them from place to place.

Spring Blooms for Both Gardens and Designs

My favorite spring flowers and shrubs, and ones that I recommend you consider for adding sheer beauty in your available space, depending upon your USDA hardiness zone, are these: azalea (*Rhododendron*), bloodroot (*Sanguinaria*), creeping phlox (*Phlox nivalis*), dogwood (*Cornus florida*), cushion spurge (*Euphorbia epithymoides*), forsythia (*Forsythia*), flowering star or tulip magnolias (*M. stellata, M. kobus*), grape hyacinths (*Muscari*), hyacinths (*Hyacinthus*), iris (*Iris*), jonquils (*Narcissus jonquilla*), lady's mantle (*Alchemilla mollis*), lilac (*Syringa vulgaris*), mountain laurel (*Kalmia latifolia*), redbud (*Cercis*), rhododendron (*Rhododendron*), snowdrops (*Galanthus*), viburnum (*Viburnum carlesii*), and weigela (*Weigela*). Violets, of course, often grow wild and bloodroot might be available from wildflower plant nurseries, if you search carefully.

All provide dramatic branches and flowers that add elegance to glass vases filled with water. Azalea, depending on the variety, and cushion spurge can usually be counted on to provide color for your arrangements at about the same time as dogwood. Remember that certain flowers are illegal to cut from the wild, so it is best to respect that and grow the needed supplies in your home gardens.

There is not an overabundance of blue flowers to grow for arranging, although good spring choices are hyacinths, grape hyacinths, iris, and columbine. Veronica is an invaluable addition to your garden, as it begins to bloom in the spring and goes right through the summer. In my garden, veronica is the perfect example of a transplanted perennial that looked sorrowful in its original place for two years and is now living happily ever after!

Spring is the perfect time of year to observe the basic structure of a garden and decide what wants to be moved to a more nurturing location. In taking the measure of your own spring-emerging bulbs and perennials, try to appreciate the color saturation provided by tulips and jonquils. It will help in assessing perennials as they start to bloom. Also, after a good look at the bare spots in your beds, imagine new texture and color combinations that will, if included, give vibrancy to future floral designs.

Visiting plant nurseries is a journey into the visual arts world. I look on these trips as stimulating, information-gathering adventures, announcing what is available in the local market. It is also a good opportunity to compare prices with mail-order catalogs. Be sure to save your plant, bulb, and seed catalogs. They are friends that provide hours of winter sustenance and continue to be invaluable reference materials, even after you have placed your orders.

A second reason to spend time "window shopping" at your favorite nurseries in the spring is to solidify ideas for new garden groupings. Remember those empty spots you found as spring's garden began to stretch and grow? Color harmony and textural interest can be measured before deciding on new additions. I employ garden center plant trays or cardboard boxes furnished for purchases as a palette and arrange choices just as I would approach a flower design, considering as well whether these beauties will also make sturdy cut flowers. When it comes to larger, bulkier trees and shrubs, garden center attendants are usually eager to answer questions and will gladly help group them according to height and growth pattern. This is an aid to your visualization process.

I always ask, on an intuitive level, which flowers, bushes, shrubs, and trees will thrive at Naramata. Usually they are the ones to which I am first attracted, so the answers are rather straightforward. Skeptics will say that I'll never know if the others would have worked for me, which is an excellent observation. I am content in the questioning, however. It is one of my ways, and I do get answers.

Apartment dwellers can design in the same manner, making gardening on the balcony or patio a more thoughtful and organized process. Collapsible, heavy-duty, woven plastic bags, made in England, are excellent for carrying flower purchases into apartment elevators. Another handy tool is a seven-foot square drop cloth made of the same material. It will protect floors and carpets while gardening indoors. Both of these are available through numerous gardening catalogs. I also use the drop cloth when working in commercial spaces to protect the floors.

Snowdrops (Leucojum)

Spring Edibles

After weeks of reading seed catalogs, planning what we will do in our gardens once winter is over, it is wonderful to be outside, getting reacquainted with the wild. Roots that have been hiding under ice, snow, and leaves send up tender shoots. Delicate woodland bloodroot liberates our sight and gives permission to start the search for healing herbs—most people call them weeds—and edible greens like winter cress *(Barbarea vulgaris)*, dandelion *(Taraxacum)*, and chicory *(Cichorium intybus)*.

Look for winter cress in fields, by stream beds, and in ditches as early as February and March. The leaves taste best while the weather is still cold. By April, the flower buds of cress are ready to be eaten, and later, when the cress is going to seed, the still-edible yellow flowers are lovely as garnish for salads and platters. After gathering greens, you might try eating them either raw or blanched.

If cooking is your preference, the following method is my favorite: *Wash the greens thoroughly, snap off any tough stem ends, and place the wet greens in a two-quart saucepan. Pour one tablespoon of olive oil over them and add three cloves of peeled and sliced garlic. Cover the pot and steam the greens until they are thoroughly wilted.*

Complementary colors spill over the edge of a terra-cotta pot wrapped in honeysuckle vines.

Leaves picked late in the season tend to be bitter. If this happens, parboil them first, drain, and proceed as above.

Dandelions bring warm memories of childhood days, racing the wind with little bunches of fuzz clutched in our fists, watching the seeds blow about as we speed to nowhere. Adults can enjoy the whole plant, as long as you pick them where herbicides and pesticides have not been applied. Dandelion greens and roots—best collected from fields and wild places—make an excellent companion for cress in your salad. Just remember that earliest spring is the best time for both, as leaves toughen when their flowers start to bloom.

Dandelions are not the only spring plants producing edible tubers. The young tubers of daylilies (*Hemerocallis*) are easily dug anytime during the year and are delicious steamed or raw. It is important to know that the shoots atop dug tubers can be replanted and will grow again quite rapidly. Later in the spring, I collect daylily buds, flowers, or even wilted blossoms, adding them to stir fry dishes and salads. They are both delicious and beautiful. Dandelion roots and leaves, which make excellent teas, are considered an overall tonic for the body. The raw leaves add a certain tartness to salads, while roots can be saved for making tinctures or teas. (Consult with a professional herbalist for specific information.)

Another healthy spring perennial is pokeweed. In the south, we call it by its familiar name—poke salad—and eat only the young green leaves. Poke should always be parboiled for ten minutes, the water tossed out, then steamed at a low temperature for another fifteen minutes. Any seasoning can be added, but I prefer garlic and olive oil as with the winter cress. Note: Poke becomes poisonous when it is more than 12 inches tall.

Chicory leaves, too, are delicate when young. I think they are best when you dig the entire plant, trimming off the root at the top with the new little leaves still attached. These can be eaten raw in salads. Chicory is easy to recognize as it matures, since later in the season its blue flowers are literally covered with butterflies. Every vegetable has its peak, and the wild ones are no exception, so be alert to their waxing and waning!

One of my favorite lunches, with ingredients partly from field and partly from garden, is a salad of mustard and winter cress flowers, spinach, and sorrel. Scrambled farm eggs, seasoned with fresh thyme, chives, and chive blossoms are a perfect accompaniment, enjoyed with a slice of toasted crusty spelt (an antique grain) bread drizzled with olive oil.

Dill, a whimsical side of the herb garden

Self expression born of creativity becomes crowning glory

Suggested ingredients for a naturally wild spring salad are:

chickweed (*Cerastium*)

dandelion greens

dandelion flowers

redbud flowers

Johnny-jump-up (*Viola tricolor*)

pansies (*Viola x wittrockiana*)

winter cress or mustard (*Brassica*) flowers. (The latter two grow close to one another, are quite similar in appearance, and can be identified easily by their leaves.)

Top with your favorite vinaigrette dressing, preferably homemade. Remember to gather these ingredients in a known, "organic" environment.

Flowering Herbal Baths

Look to the herb garden for adding more to your life than just seasoning for meals. Nothing is better than a nice warm bath, enhanced with those same herbs. I especially enjoy a wonderful soak after a day of gardening, as well as in the wee hours of a wakeful morning. It is doubly luxurious with fresh garden fragrances added to the warm water. Going out to the garden at four o'clock in the morning to gather rosemary (*Rosmarinus officinalis*) is an ordinary occurrence in this household.

Since all of the rooms, including the bath, have uncurtained glass French doors, the tub provides a year-round orchestra seat for observing Nature's show. Sometimes, when the early dawn view of Hidden Valley is illuminated by a full moon, I feel included in the natural order of happenings just outside the door. Deer are still at their browsing, the raccoon wishes he could open the bird feeder, a red fox heads home from the hunt, and birds begin their morning song. In April, I see the goldfinches turn golden again, their feathers losing winter's homely brown tinge.

Fragrant lavender (*Lavandula*) and calming chamomile (*Chamaemelum nobilis*) oils, leafy stems of lemon balm (*Melissa officinalis*), rosemary, and peppermint (*Mentha piperita*) are favorite additions to the warm water. There is also joy in collecting them.

If you wish to make herbal bath oils, you will find simple directions in the Winter chapter. Alternatively, soothing and healing oils, such as almond and grapeseed, can be purchased at health foods stores, if you prefer not to make your own.

Herbs can be used as natural pest repellents, too. Many times in the summer when gnats, flies, or no-see-'ems are bothersome in the garden, I'll pin sprigs of lavender to my work clothes. Another deterrent is my gnat-hat: ribbons, about six inches long attached to the brim of a straw hat move about as I garden, discouraging little winged creatures from getting in eyes, ears, and nose.

Après gardening is a time for comfrey *(Symphytum)*, calendula *(Calendula)*, rosemary, and lemon balm. All are a comfort to moisture-deprived hands. Since it is also a great first aid for cut fingers, I keep a tube of calendula ointment in my work kit as well. Creams made from aloe vera, clover blossoms, chamomile, calendula, comfrey, avocado, and rosemary are also commercially available.

Flowering Hats

One of my favorite workshops is hat making, and spring is the time for wearing beautiful hats. During this workshop, everyone creates a one-of-a-kind, flower-bedecked hat.

Starting with a variety of unadorned hats, ranging from baseball caps to large-brimmed straw styles, each person decides on her color preferences. The selection of ornaments, ribbons, fabrics, silk flowers, and fruits chosen by each workshop participant naturally follows. Carefully choosing and finally affixing just the right items to reflect each person's special personality gives genuine pleasure and amusement.

When a woman puts on a beautiful hat, her being changes before your eyes. She stands straighter, her body becomes conscious that she is Woman. Her eyes sparkle, she admires herself in the mirror, not vaingloriously, but seeing and appreciating herself in a whole new way. There is a bending, a softening, almost a dance between her figure and the partner of reflection; the head turns this way and that, the hands adjust the chapeau just so, then readjust once again.

By creating a hat geared to each participant's idea of self, hat-making workshops allow that special something hidden within to emerge spontaneously. No one disappears behind the "I-just-don't-wear-hats" ploy to deny herself such a joyful experience! Women who explore this workshop invariably telephone afterwards to tell of unexpected results: all their friends loved seeing them in self-proclaiming hats.

Spring hat workshops manage to free the spirit for what some consider a more formal experience: that of flower designing.

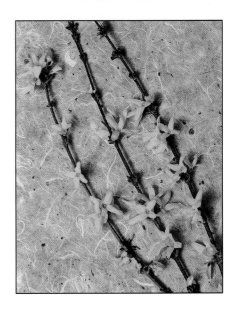

Celebrating Earth Day with Butterflies

In spring, everyone wants to entertain, and the twenty-fifth anniversary celebration of Earth Day at Airlie House in Warrenton, Virginia, presented a challenging flower design project.

*The mechanics of our spring arrangement
include a terra-cotta pot and saucer, a
papier-mâché liner, two blocks of standard
floral foam, davey tape, and a knife
for cutting stems.*

*First I trimmed the corners of the
floral foam to assure a snug fit in the
papier-mâché liner. After soaking, the
blocks are set vertically into the liner,
secured by davey tape. Vertical placement
insures proper "wicking," the continued
absorption of water.*

*Previous page: Boxes of ribbons
and silk flowers invite the adventurous to
imagine new possibilities for textured,
colorful hat fixings.*

The theme for the entire Earth Day weekend was butterflies, in honor of Roger Tory Peterson, a naturalist-artist
famous the world over for his field guides and environmental
activism. The opening dinner offered a unique opportunity to
work out botanically-correct centerpieces keyed to the life cycle
of a butterfly.

For more than three hundred guests, seated at twenty-five
round tables, the dining room was transformed into a country
flower garden, complete with candlelight and centerpieces of
four-foot-tall dogwood blossoms, arranged individually with
various herbs, vegetables, and flowers dear to the hearts of
butterflies. Painted balsa wood butterflies fluttered overhead,
energized by the heat from human bodies, rather than the usual
solar-power. (In addition to the centerpieces in the dining room
celebrating butterflies, four large arrangements of butterfly-ori-
ented materials were placed in the public areas of Airlie House.)

Since all of the arrangements were to be sold after the dinner as part of the weekend's benefit activities, the baskets had

Forsythia is inserted three inches into the wet floral foam. The upward thrust of the branches adds a woodsy feel and defines the parameters of the final piece, an asymmetrical arrangement. To keep the branches from twisting about, I "squared off" the ends with my knife before inserting them in the foam. Dried honeysuckle vines swirl around the terra-cotta pot.

Lilac stems of differing length are grouped together to give impact. The shortest stems have the largest blooms and sit deeply into the arrangement. I squared off these woody stems with my knife before inserting them in the floral foam, as with the forsythia, for stability.

to hold up to major handling. This was accomplished by taping floral foam into the baskets, as well as wiring logs, rocks, and tall branches securely in place. Lemon leaf *(Salal)* and viburnum leaves gave visual weight at the base of each arrangement and served to hide the mechanics. Lavender petunia *(Petunia)* and orange marigold *(Tagetes)* seedlings were actually planted in the basket liners, and yellow hybrid lilies, pink verbena, rosemary, ageratum, and cut broccoli were added at the last. Both sheet and deer moss placed at the feet of the flowers created a woodsy look.

In making the arrangements for Earth Day as ecologically correct for butterflies as possible, there was one ingredient excluded from the dining room at Airlie House: a butterfly puddle. In the wild, butterflies prefer clearings, rather than inhabiting deep woods; thus their love of gardens. They need water and happily congregate in and around what we might call mud puddles found in garden paths or driveways.

Our Spring Arrangement

In the fifteenth century, spring green dye was produced from a rare pigment. Today, we still relate the color to signs of rebirth in Nature. Bells of Ireland speak of this green. Their color and the pink of the Van Dyke tulips complement each other, adding animation to the design. Lavender lilacs extend the complementary pattern, while energy is stepped up another notch by the hot-peach azaleas. Forced forsythia branches "outreach" to form a delicate framework while tiny flowerets of lilac present a pebble-like surface in contrast to the silken tulips. Bells of Ireland, prickly to the touch, invite scrutiny of the circular excursion of blossoms around their stems. Azaleas look upward as they encourage the viewer to walk into springtime. This arrangement is about color, movement, and texture, as befits any imaginary April extravaganza!

Tulips are a bit wayward. Their singularity of character is charming—the more precocious, the better. If, however, a design requires that they straighten up, wrap the entire bunch in paper and place their stem ends in deep, warm water. After several hours of drinking, their "posture" will improve. For this arrangement I decided to encourage the vivacity of the tulips. They were settled into the composition after I studied the directional purpose of each flower head. Adding movement, grace, and humor, they are also a perfect spring pink. They are arranged in clusters like the lilacs and bells of Ireland.

In the completed spring arrangement bells of Ireland are a perfect tonic for the lavender lilacs. Their intricacies give weight and width to the arrangement, proportionate to the height. This animated design invites the viewer to "participate" by noticing the contrasting textures and vivid colors.

A word of caution about the care that must be taken with spring greens. Most are practically impossible to use, as the new growth is so tender that it wilts easily, especially in floral foam; experiment when conditioning your foliage to see what will work best for you, as material availability may differ depending on geographical area and the type of plantings found in your gardens.

Final Thoughts about the Spring Season

In spring, we expect an orderly progression of bloom. The pace increases in woodlands, meadows, and parks as vibrant colors and the luscious bright greens of trees miraculously appear, cheered on by joyful birdsong. Next, the dazzling depth of color and the wealth of our own gardens reward us for all those hours of autumn gardening.

Bells of Ireland (Moluccella laevis), *tulips* (Tulipa), *lilacs* (Syringa), *forsythia* (Forsythia), *azalea* (Rhododendron 'Dorothy Gish')

I cut the stems of azalea blossoms short, using their starlike faces to reinforce the dynamics of their complementary spring-like color. They function as a disguise for the mechanics and lead the eye through the arrangement.

Spring can surprise with its capriciousness. One day we are yearning for springtime and the next day a rush of undiluted color from every corner of the forest, meadow, and garden calls out, "Good morning!" The effect on me is twofold. First, I have an irresistible desire to just sit in the immediate splendor of this ephemeral beauty, letting it fill my senses, traveling throughout my entire being. Secondly, my wish is to gather great armloads of branches bearing multitudes of color-filled blossoms to bring indoors. On all counts, the variety of forms in which Nature clothes herself puts me in a state of reverence, more so in spring than at any other time.

With a freshening of the spirit, the desire to share the feelings with friends and students is undeniable. Sitting under flowering branches, be they inside the house or inside the woods, I am cradled in a colorful network of Nature's arms. It seems that the earth holds us close, nurturing us awake after the hiatus of winter.

Since spring has been exceptionally dry this year in Madison County, I am grateful for every raindrop that graces the land. It is that same old childhood feeling of wanting to rush outside to greet a storm, just standing there—being part of the rain as it performs miracles of transformation. These are luxuries not available at the corner market. For this reason, I always resent the attitudes of those who groan whenever there is a dark cloud in the sky. This includes weather forecasters who make a science of doom from a day or two of beneficial showers bent on feeding the earth and our thirsty young flowers and vegetables. Perhaps those of us who live with well water appreciate rainwater more. For those who have not had reason to realize that rain bestows health on us all, maybe it is a novel idea to consider. The earth and we, going along with the belief that we are part of a whole, require it to survive.

There is
no creation
that does not have a radiance,
be it greenness or seed,
blossom or beauty.
It could not be creation without it.

——Hildegard of Bingen

SUMMER

In summer, more than in any other season, we need only go to gardens, forests, parks, mountains, or shore to reestablish our spiritual connection with Nature's quiet and bounty, as well as her unexpected dramas.

In summer, we are able to feel the ways of Nature. We find comfort and beauty reflected in our daily lives by flowing with her patterns, thus living in a way complementary to both the earth and ourselves. This connection, once established, alerts us to change. We become observers, we live the rainstorms, wind, and drought that rearrange our part of the earth. Personal patterns change. No matter how avidly we plan and plant, we bend to the influence of a greater force.

In summer, animals, birds, and insects directly affect our lives. At Naramata, hummingbirds fly through the open kitchen door, attracted by colors that promise nectar, while a black bear lumbers through the meadow at teatime, on the prowl for woodland berries. As I watch, a willing participant, fresh questions arise, important to the pattern of summer life: "How do I get the hummingbirds off the ceiling fan?" "Should I wait until just a little later in the afternoon to take my walk?"

A lily growing by the front door welcomes guests, with its fragrance and color, to the dinner table just inside. Queen Anne's lace fills a corner of the meadow, now a landing pad for lightning bugs, and later the fragile framework preceding patches of vibrant blue wild lobelia that spring from the edges of a moist streambed. Summer defines and softens patterns, making us part of the joyful creation around us. Her flowers, like a beautiful smile, bring inner gladness.

Blue delphinium (Delphinium), assorted country roses, and Italian ruscus (Ruscus)

A casual note is struck with florist delphinium and country roses as they spill over the edges of an antique tin ice-cream freezer. They suggest both summer's cool shadows and the warmth of vivid hues.

I angled branches of roses towards the center of the tin, interweaving stems for security. (Thorns left on the stems tend to catch on others, helping to anchor the materials.) Medium and tall stems of delphinium followed. Lastly positioned were the longest roses, evoking airiness. Italian ruscus from the florist gives the composition an ephemeral quality.

Gathering summer grasses

The Promise of Summer

For me, summer begins when field grasses are in full bloom and the first hay is cut. Mown clover used in red clover blossom tea or steeped for medicinal tinctures also is more easily collected at that time.

After the first sweet meadow hay is mowed in June, I gather fresh summer grasses for use in impromptu flower arrangements later in the year. I tie the grasses in neat bundles with baling twine and hang them upside down in my gardening shed to dry. As the grasses shrink from loss of moisture, I tighten the twine to keep the bundles secure.

Only when there is a rattling sound as you shake the grasses in your hand is it time to roll the cut hay into huge, thousand-pound bales. If the weather is fine, mowing and baling will take a total of three or four days. From the point of view of preserving wildlife, it is better to wait until the end of June for a first cutting, so that bird nestlings down in the fields have an opportunity to mature and fly from secreted nests in the wildflowers, grasses, and clover.

The passage into a new season feels complete when the rolled bales of hay stand majestically in the fields, looking for all the world as if the Great Sculptor arranged them according to His own sense of aesthetics.

My main goal in moving far from a city environment was to cultivate a life enriched by health-giving fresh air, well water, homegrown vegetables, and peace. I was fully aware that—as humans—we do try to control our environment; so I promised to ask myself continually whether the alterations and additions made to accommodate my new home and gardens would be consistent with the well-being of this land. That is an ongoing process. I find daily companionship with wild things and am never more aware of having made the right decision than in the full lushness of a Virginia summer.

A remote country setting seems the perfect place to experience summer's ever changing ways of saying, "Good morning!" The unexpected simply occurs. Summer greetings are there in the city, too, but sometimes you need to be more on the alert if you wish to incorporate these surprises into your life.

Starting down the drive one June morning, my car was suddenly encircled by what looked like an acre of baby turkeys! Their alarmed flight was followed an instant later by a lumbering turkey nursemaid. Did all those babies belong to this mother? There were so many that the low-hanging tree branches were soon filled with future Thanksgiving dinners.

Later that same week, just as the sun was deciding to call it a day, the classic hare and tortoise race was reenacted at a bend in the drive. Spying my car, the neighborhood rabbit raced for the underbrush, while I encouraged his plodding competitor into the field, a less life-threatening environment. Even here, driveways are suicidal raceways for someone so vulnerable.

These encounters, common among animals, can teach us that coexistence between the species is a message for humanity. Struggling to understand all that Nature teaches, we witness events in the country and in our own backyards, especially if we decide to encourage and preserve even the smallest wild areas on our land.

Awareness comes to people who visit Naramata, or so they report. Acknowledgment of their own already existing naturalistic environments in city or suburb gives permission to enhance these areas, hoping for a return to a less complicated way of life.

We are healthier when we live consciously, and this includes every facet of our lives. Well-cared-for flowers and vegetables are an example because they in turn nourish us. What is called The Law of Similars goes into effect: like attracts like. As we

begin, even in the tiniest way, to respect and work within the laws of Nature, Nature responds instantly and serves graciously in ways we could never anticipate. When she seems harsh, we should question the reasons and look to the long view, rather than acknowledging only the present and evident.

A Flood Across the Land

Crows mostly travel in air wing formations, their raucous, demanding gossip hard to miss when they are in the neighborhood. It is rare to suddenly see a lone crow, gliding silently, carefully examining a drastically altered landscape. Where once below there had been a stream, hidden by underbrush, he now sees a dramatic waterfall spilling into a newly sunken pool that, in turn, flows into a shallow silt pond exactly the depth for a proper crow bath. He plunges recklessly downward into this newly formed pond to bathe and splash. The splendid, shiny bird emerges preening and strutting onto a jagged, teardrop-shaped rock formation called an alluvial fan; it was formed by rocks washing down the mountainside.

Madison County, Virginia, like so much of this part of the state, was changed on June 27, 1995, when a deluge of thirteen inches of rain fell within a period of twelve hours. It flooded the land. Water, cascading down the mountainsides, heaved great boulders and trees down ravines and hollows, into valleys and onto unsuspecting farmland and houses below. My neighbor's driveway, one hundred yards in length, was covered by seven hundred tons of rock.

Nature will have her way. The runs, streams, creeks, and rivers dramatically overran their banks, carrying everything in their path miles downstream. Bridges were washed out; roads collapsed; homes were destroyed.

Hillsides became waterfalls, and silt settled in the bottom land, rerouting formerly peaceful waterways. Culverts, supposedly large enough to handle fifty-year floods, were filled and buried under tons of silt and debris. Where there were once views of familiar serenity, the valley now looked, to that high-flying crow, like a great African plain.

I was one of the lucky ones. When the rains finally ended, the house stood unscathed, though the upper driveway was awash in a sea of red mud. While my perennial gardens near the house remained undisturbed, the lower gardens consisting of raised vegetable beds and circular beds for annuals were another story. They were eroded and waterlogged. The middle portion of the upper meadow had become a maelstrom of crashing boulders and angry rushing waters. Lower fields and driveway were

Phlox (Phlox paniculata), *hybrid lilies* (Lilium), *yarrow* (Achillea mille-folium), *blackberry lily* (Belamcanda chinesis), *roses* (Rosa) *on arbor, and Moonbeam coreopsis* (Coreopsis verticillata)

Perennials, bulbs, tubers, and an "arbored" climbing rose frame the nearby foothill. Moonbeam coreopsis serves as underglow for the yarrow and hybrid lilies while phlox and blackberry lily take a back seat.

During a walk through the garden
with clippers in hand, I often respond to
impromptu choices such as this
combination of colors and textures settled
comfortably into a narrow-necked vase.
By encouraging the trailing qualities of
both buddleia and leucothoe, I added a
sense of grace to the more upright flowers.

changed into a river of many deltas formed by silt and rocks, strewn with trees denuded of all foliage, branches, and bark.

All of us in the region began the task of deciding what to rebuild and what to leave alone. We clearly heard the message: Nature is in charge. In personal efforts to beautify and carve a small niche in this grand universe comes a consciousness of the fact that the planet belongs first to Nature. Trying creatively to gentle the obvious impact of the flood here on this land called Naramata, I became aware of—and part of—new patterns, patterns that would become the beauty of land washed clean by Divine Forces.

As I look back to the time of the flood, the evidence is clear. My aging pile of hardwood mulch lies near the banks of one of the downflowing mountain streams that raged out of bounds during those June days. The treasured mulch, gold to me, lay in the path of the swollen rush of water and tumbling rocks. Amazingly, having separated itself in two above that store of brown gold, the waters rejoined themselves just below, turning the pile itself into a small island. Awareness is one of the steps in developing harmony with our environment. Upon recognizing what might be called a "pattern of protection," it is no wonder I feel safety at Naramata. I try to care for this land, and Nature gives recognition of the fact.

Summer's Ripening Garden

The heightening of summer brings lushness to the garden. With June, hollyhock (*Alcea*) stalks grow taller and roses become abundant, Casa Blanca lilies (*Lilium* 'Casa Blanca') welcome all comers with fragrance at the front steps. In rapid succession, the mid-June astilbes (*Astilbe*), lavenders (*Lavandula*), feverfew (*Chrysanthemum parthenium*), and hybrid lilies (*Lilium*) replace the roses (*Rosa*) and peonies (*Paeonia*) that had dominated the late spring garden with their vibrant colors and textures. Columbine (*Aquilegia*) begins to wane in the summer heat while clematis (*Clematis*) dramatizes one of the arbors. Clove pinks (*Dianthus caryophyllus*) are a must-have for the summer garden. From a bank above the house, they bring fragrance to an entire acre of land and adore blooming. Cut them to enjoy their heady perfume indoors and do remember to shear them back after they bloom. Add a bit of manure, and they will come into full flower again. Plant, cut, and enjoy.

The trailing garden honeysuckle (*Lonicera etrusca* 'Superba') already needs pruning. Its tentacles so imprison the wind chimes overhead that they cease to make music. Wild honeysuckle vines (*L. japonica*) greet homecomings with fragrance so sweet that I pause to inhale deeply, momentarily motionless and reminded of the precious ginger blossoms native to Hawaii! Fences and forest edges are overgrown with this imported Oriental honeysuckle, sweet-smelling, invasive, and exceedingly usable. The vines in the hedgerow shelter birds, providing places for their nests, where they nurture their young and from which they sing and chatter in the early mornings.

Nicotiana (Nicotiana), *celosia* (Celosia), *sunflowers* (Helianthus), *and zinnias* (Zinnia)

A long view of the house from the driveway shows the raised vegetable and circular annual beds near the grape arbor. After the 1995 flood, I had to sow seeds three times in the annual beds. Only at the end of that weather-turbulent summer did they begin to look confident.

Choosing the "uninhabited" spots, I cut abundant armloads of honeysuckle. As material for arranging, it is unsurpassed and holds up better in the spring and early summer than much of the new green growth of the garden. It trails elegantly from most any place you can think to use it, from a bud vase to a whole mantelpiece. It can also be cut and twined into tiny rings or large circles that, tied securely and hung to dry, will be used later in the fall and winter as bases for wreaths or unrolled as garlands. Tiny ones can be used to decorate Christmas trees, huge ones to decorate barn doors.

July is a time to continue harvesting grasses for use in the fall and winter, along with dried columbine pods, crocosmia (*Crocosmia*) seedheads, all varieties of yarrow (*Achillea millefolium*),

Siberian iris pods *(Iris sibirica)*, and some early hydrangeas *(Hydrangea)*. These last I let stay on the bush ("harden off") for four to six weeks after bloom time, watching for changes in or deepening of color before cutting them.

Notice what you see in Nature's patterns and in your own gardens. Feel their energies and memorize what is before you. What better example can we have for creating flower arrangements? When designs are based on your observations of Nature at work, your own version of harmony and balance can be created with confidence. The result is called beauty.

Consider what happens to people who move into old houses with neglected gardens. Very often, they discover delightful antique shrubs, trees, bulbs, reseeding annuals, and hardy perennials, not to mention stray tomato or squash vines and perhaps overgrown areas of who-knows-what hidden in those gardens. They have inherited the legacy of some other gardener's dream, time, and effort.

Of course, it isn't always easy to see what is there, especially for the less experienced, but enthusiastic gardener. It takes time, exploration, and care to find the real treasures. Many times after using unusual materials in a workshop, I'll get a phone call from a participant saying, "I just found that shrub in my garden." This is a thrilling moment for the two of us; it proves the value of fresh vision, a vision that inevitably is shared. It multiplies exponentially. My riches often come from the discoveries of others.

There is really no great difference, when you look at it, between gardening on ten acres or gardening in containers— except a great deal more work. All of the same design considerations apply: scale (ultimate height and breadth), color (monochromatic or contrasting, bright or pastel), texture (velvety, shaggy, delicate, rough), shape (round, starlike, oval, spiky, clusters.) Your *vision* brings these elements together successfully. This is the most important ingredient in both flower and garden design planning and execution—no matter what the scale. Let yourself dream, visualize the impossible, the outrageous, the unattainable, and see the beautiful in your mind's eye. Figure out a time frame for accomplishing your dream and a workable budget for ordering plants, bulbs, and seeds. By bringing joy to your bit of the earth, your investment of time, effort, and money will be rewarded for years to come. All of your achievements, like a beacon, reach out to nourish those about you.

Organic matter (compost), nontoxic fertilizers (such as manure and kelp derivatives), builder's sand, and peat moss will enrich your soil, while mulch (straw or twice-shredded hard-

Brilliant arrays of butterfly weed (Asclepias tuberosa) *attract butterflies wearing equally vibrant showy summer garb. The meadows teem with butterflies pleasuring themselves at nectar-laden wildflowers.*

Favorite summer roses

wood) helps the soil to retain moisture and keeps the roots of plants cool. You will need tools that fit into your hands comfortably and are powerful enough to do their job, making your work easier and more efficient.

While perennials, shrubs, and trees have grown exceptionally well this year, I've noticed that it has been a "bad lettuce year." My experimental grain crops, amaranth and quinoa grown from heirloom seeds, along with all of the annuals and vegetables, were washed out by the flood. I was especially sorry to lose the amaranth and quinoa. Both were new to me this year and, because it takes a longer time for them to mature, the season was too advanced to replant either. However, the thrice-planted zinnias (*Zinnia*), nicotiana (*Nicotiana*), sunflowers (*Helianthus*), and marigolds (*Tagetes*) made repeated efforts and became luxuriant in September, having struggled through cycles of being both overly wet and overly dry in their straw-separated rows.

Slugs and snails sleep in the nurturing straw by day and forage at night, dining ritualistically on zinnias just as they reach the two-inch sprout stage. I retaliate by using the time-honored remedy of placing large saucers of beer in the beds in hopes of intoxicating and drowning them. The operation has been a success—as long as the beer supplies do not evaporate in the sun! Diatomaceous earth scattered in the rows also discourages slugs and snails by abrading their skins, but it must be reapplied each time it rains.

Summer Surprises

If spring is the time that animals and other creatures awaken and begin to move about, summer is definitely the time they take to the high roads . . . at least on this land.

Besides the expected blackberries of summer, there is a near relative to the raspberry that proliferates in our foothills. The local folk call them wineberries, for they are round, rich, and beautifully rose red. I call them "bear berries" because just about the time they are ripening in July, I usually see a bear on the prowl. Bears habitually come down out of Shenandoah National Park for an evening's repast.

It seems that the grape arbor is just as attractive to bears as the wild wineberries are. This arbor is a sturdy rectangular frame mounted on five-foot timbers. Sapling trees are braided across the top of the structure so that the spring vines weave between them, providing strength for the coming clusters of grapes.

I awoke one morning to see sagging vines, their supports lying on the ground. Branches on the young peach tree growing next to the arbor were twisted and bent. The small tree was

timidly wearing her first crop of almost-ripe peaches. Using my imagination, I visualized an eager bear, drawn in by the sweet scent of grapes, lumbering down the field to the arbor, hidden by the safety of nightfall. The peach tree must have seemed a handy ladder, but proved unable to carry such weight. The lower branches were bent to the ground and partially snapped from the bear's weight as he climbed toward his goal. The latticed saplings atop the grape arbor splintered like twigs as the bear fell through to the ground, entangled in vines. Or maybe the bear climbed the arbor to reach the peaches, stretching for slender limbs as the arbor gave way under his weight. However it happened, it must have been funny, though not to the bear and not to me, at first. Later on, after regaining a sense of humor, I wasn't sure which disappointed me more—the sabotage done to the tree and arbor or the fact that I had missed being an eyewitness to the escapades of the perpetrator!

Whether it's deciding what we will actually grow or how we will deal with the vagaries of Nature, gardeners are immersed in preparation and work the year round. The truth of summertime, however, always brings unpredictable delights of which we never dreamed when our gardens were just in the planning stages.

I am often asked where to begin in planning table settings for a party. Our picnic is a perfect example. First, I selected a quilt to provide harmony as background for the strong colors of summer edibles. Old handwrought wooden bowls and a blue stencilled ice-cream freezer are perfect complements for the antique quilt. Flowers were chosen to "match" the quilt. To display the cherry tomatoes, I filled the oversized bowl with crumpled newspaper covered by layers of green leaves in which to nest the tomatoes.

A bold early dahlia

*A grindstone from an old mill is
the center "stone" of the Indian Medicine
Wheel I built in back of the house. It is
surrounded by several varieties of thyme*
(Thymus praecox), *primarily creeping
thyme which has purplish flowers in late
spring and early summer. The fragrance
emanating from the thyme as it is crushed
underfoot is one of my favorite
summer aromas.*

As an example, at the end of last summer, I noticed a new, tiny butterfly bush *(Buddleia davidii)*. It could only have been planted by a bird, because birds and I are the only ones who landscape here at Naramata! This unplanned member of the garden is growing by one of the arbors behind the house. It stands next to the Indian Medicine Wheel (a circular formation of rocks built around four main stones, each facing the Four Directions). Flanking the Medicine Wheel are the arbors, constructed of young dogwood saplings and offering cozy retreats for birds and people. Sunflowers, also contributed by my winged gardener friends, and self-seeding cosmos *(Cosmos bipinnatus)* from years past have now joined the butterfly bush. Four varieties of scented thymes *(Thymus)* and other herbs grow between the stones of the Medicine Wheel. This grouping is a new miniature habitat for bees, butterflies, and hummingbirds. All pleasure themselves not only at the colorful cosmos and sunflowers but also at the nectar-filled honeysuckle blossoms twining through one of the arbors. Several bird-feeding stations grace the area, attractions for nestlings and their parents.

With the extra June rain and heat this year, all of the perennials, bulbs, shrubs, and trees at Naramata experienced major growth. The "unexpected" butterfly bush is a prime example. It is now nine feet tall and still growing. In fact, a jasmine vine *(Gelsemium sempervirens)*—its yellow flowers an excellent source for homeopathic remedies—planted at the side of the honeysuckle-covered arbor is being overrun by these new garden attractions. I decided early on to observe this example of earthly competition with interest rather than interfere through preferential weeding out.

The challenge of working with Nature as a partner is a process of continual reward and frustration, but one that provides experience in flexible thinking and problem solving. We learn, even when faced with major "rearrangements," like floods, when to take action and when to leave things alone.

Find Your Earth Connection

One of my favorite summer creatures has to be the spider. There is a superabundance of them around Naramata, and their many disguises are astonishing.

There is a spider to match almost every flower: chrome yellow ones for marigolds and goldenrod, reddish brown ones that hide in the hot-colored zinnias and Mexican sunflowers, green ones everywhere, and those that ride into the house on garden or field flowers. They venture inside to do their own decorating, weaving gossamer patterns around chair and table legs.

Those lacy webs are a complex visual puzzle if you spy one just as the sun is angling its morning self into an open meadow. Webs hang between flower stalks, become rooftops to low-growing grasses, and swing in a seemingly precarious position from dry June grasses. Some take the shape of lacework baskets, others are two-dimensional; some detain struggling crickets momentarily, others are successful snares for the occupant spider's breakfast.

One day, when I arrived to work on the flowers at the Airlie Center, a friend reached over, took a single spider thread from my wrist, and played with the spider as one would a yo-yo, until he got that spider back to safety in the outside world.

Even younger gardeners are fascinated with my arachnid adornments. A young boy attending a children's class gently lifted a hobo spider that was traveling on my sleeve—no doubt to help me unload flowers from the car—and quietly took it off

At sunrise a Naramata spider rests after his duties on the night shift.

Casa Blanca lilies (Lilium 'Casa Blanca'), *chief greeters at my front door, gathered into a favorite Victorian pitcher.*

to a corner of the room. I watched, realizing there was communication between the two. As his interest waned, he respectfully took the little fellow outside. Placing it gingerly on a leaf, he admonished the spider to go back and play with its own friends now. As the class progressed, this incident led to a discussion not only of spiders, but also of the shrub playing host to a newfound playmate.

One-to-one communication with things natural gives the feeling of an earth connection. I remember one early morning spent collecting red clover blossoms (*Trifolium incarnatum*) on an embankment above the front porch. The freshly gathered blossoms were to be the essential ingredient in an herbal tincture, the making of which was new to me. Deciding that a completely full mason jar would be the right quantity of blossom heads, I set out

Hardie's Recipe for Red Clover Tincture
Pack a mason jar tightly and to the top with blossom heads. Fill the jar with vodka and let the tincture steep for six weeks, preferably where the moonlight will nurture it. Remove the blossoms and use the tincture as prescribed by your herbal practitioner.

with jar in hand. My "developing" recipe required three ingredients: the mason jar, the clover blossoms, and my own soon-to-be-discovered picking style. The beginnings were awkward: climbing the embankment, plucking fresh blossom heads, shifting the glass jar from hand to hand. After trial and error, I finally ended up holding the jar between my feet. This way, the blossom heads no longer tumbled out of the jar as I picked away on the slope. Birds, watching over these activities, sang arias in my ears.

The task of picking took longer than expected (most enjoyable ones do!), during which the early morning birdsong and I became inseparable. Naramata is tranquility. A sense of gratitude for the gifts inherent in the place gave way to the certainty that this land takes care of me. I belong.

Patterns

Have you ever noticed the curvilinear nature of Nature? As I see it, flowers tend to be round and soft or spiky and assertive, and each adds dimension and texture to flower beds. Earthly curves seem especially abundant in the summer, when Nature is at her most sensuous. Animal paths in the woods, for example, snake about; they never go straight uphill, but always meander along, changing course with the topography. Animals know that traversing a hillside is more energy-efficient than climbing vertically. Water chases itself down the foothill, doing switchbacks, taking whimsical turns at times, always following the path of least resistance. These patterns are more visible in the winter, but the making of them seems a summer occurrence.

Fish follow the identical pattern, undulating through meadow streams, darting gracefully about in little pools. Fig Newton, my cat, brushes through the garden with those same graceful movements, in tune with silent rhythms, taking a

straight course only if in pursuit, as do other animals bent on the chase. Hawks drift and dip with the wind currents, and goldfinches move through the air as if they were surf topping.

As the crow flies, straight lines are more of a people thing. Squares, rectangles, triangles: these are the shapes that contain our living spaces and some gardens. They are not the real shapes of comfort. Many-petaled flowers beckon us with their open and welcoming faces the same way that soft furnishings in our homes cushion our bodies. Stunning sweeps and flowering shapes rest us, whether they are in interior furnishings, favorite paintings, fields of vision, or in our flower designs. Their soothing rhythms bring peace to overly busy lives and comfort to our hungry souls. The source is unending, especially in summer gardens. Take notice of the rounded heads of sunflowers, the many-petaled marigold faces, the cosmos that nod their heads in the late-summer evening, or the rose petals that have fallen onto a stony path.

A "Jewel" of a Weed

For people who are instantaneous poison ivy catchers, jewelweed is the weed to know. Available in liquid form at most health food stores, jewelweed is an everyday summer remedy for those of us who live in the country. It can actually be found growing right next to its companion plant, poison ivy; I have often heard that poisonous plants and their antidote are usually planted by Nature in the same vicinity.

Once you have been "introduced" to jewelweed, the leaf is easily recognizable, and its late summer orchid-like orange flowers make it simple to spot.

Jewelweed's two- to four-foot tall bushy stalks grow plentifully along lightly shaded stream banks or in wild places. It even grows down by the lilac bushes (*Syringa vulgaris*) on one corner of the back porch—a ready-to-use pharmacy!

To use jewelweed, I mash the entire stalk thoroughly in my hands, including leaves and flowers, until my bare hands turn green, then anoint the patches of skin that are bubbling with poison ivy blisters. The juice and green plant material are messy, but it's worth it. Use jewelweed as a preventative if you think you have been exposed to poison ivy or as a topical treatment to counteract the itching and swelling of that noxious weed. Stems of jewelweed can also be kept in plastic bags in the refrigerator for successive applications.

Lilies (Lilium), *artemisia*
(Artemisia ludoviciana *'Silver-king'*),
and viburnum (Viburnum carlesii)

*It took me only fifteen minutes to
"do" this arrangement from cutting to
finishing. I placed the flowers into a vase
filled with warm water and bleach
"preservative" immediately after cutting,
eliminating the conditioning process.
After establishing a location for the lower
two lilies and the gray foliaged artemisia,
I then added the remaining greens,
grasses and Viburnum carlesii berries.
By establishing a support system with the
shorter flowers, I gave stability to
the longer stems.*

Arranging Summer's Bounty

I believe the "unarranged" look in flower design better reflects
our connectedness with earth. This is not to discount the value,
use, and execution of more formal, planned arrangements.
Informality tends to give free license in the use of materials,
allowing personal flair to develop into individualistic style.
One method of working toward this goal in your designs is
to carefully note what you find attractive in beautiful natural
surroundings: What better time to do that than in summer,
when the world gives us such abundance?

Observe how grasses, wildflowers, and understory shrubs
form gradual stairsteps to the towering trees. Note also that
trees tend to be generally more delicate and airy at their tops,
while the heavier lower branches reach out in a welcoming horizontal gesture. This is the same look we strive for in arrangements—more visual weight at the base of the design, gradually
allowing airiness and openness as we work the flowers and
branches upward.

Two of the most frequently asked questions in my workshops are: "Where do I begin?" and "How do a I select a container?"

Begin by selecting the flowers and other materials you wish to arrange. Next, look at the containers you have on hand. In choosing one that will complement the type of materials you have selected, ask yourself two more questions: "Where will this arrangement be used?" and "Will I need to move it?" The answers to these two questions will help you select not only the right container but also the best method for holding the flowers in place.

If your arrangement is destined to grace a dining room table and never be moved, its moorings—floral foam or poultry wire—can be less secure than for an arrangement that must be transported. When you are using a glass or crystal container, the design will be more attractive without these unsightly mechanics. The photograph of tools in Chapter I will show you the way to place tape across the tops of vases to provide stability for flower stems.

In selecting an appropriate container, choose one that coordinates well with the surroundings in which it will be placed, remembering that it must be sturdy enough to hold the required number of flowers. If you are starting a collection, purchase a few basic shapes and sizes such as the following:

Glass vases (six to ten inches tall). Ginger jar shapes are graceful and easy to work with.

Glass cylinders (ten to sixteen inches tall, five inches to seven inches in diameter).

Terra-cotta pots and saucers in all sizes. Remember that you'll need plastic or papier-mâché liners to prevent leakage.

Baskets of all shapes and sizes. The same waterproofing cautions apply.

Round or rectangular containers (approximately four by seven inches). These can be as plain as clear glass Pyrex baking dishes and loaf pans. The container will be hidden by greens and flowers placed at the base of your arrangement.

Finally, when you are more certain of your preferences, seek out antique and junk shops. There will be appealing pitchers, compotes, bowls, cachepots, and who knows what other enchantments to inspire you and add interest to your home even when they are empty!

There are so many variables that it is wise to take containers home on approval to make certain you are satisfied with selections. This is where vision once again comes into play. Learn to trust your own "eye" rather than depending on the opinion of others.

The gardening shed, dominated by old windows whose glass panes wear years of unscraped paint, is softened by florist geranium (Pelargonium zonale), caladium (Caladium), and potted impatiens (Impatiens). Lamb's ears (Stachys byzantina) and oregano (Origanum vulgare) border the path.

Children grasp the idea of companion plantings in the garden and learn that some flower and vegetable root systems are not congenial if planted too close together. They begin to wonder how these flowers we are arranging grew in the first place.

Gardening with a young companion adds richness to life. Start off with fast-growing plants, both vegetables and flowers, such as lettuce, carrots, or zinnias, if you have a garden plot. I can guarantee children will be attentive to their part of the garden and will anxiously await the time they can harvest a real crop and cut their own flowers for arranging.

If outdoor space is not available, give children wheat grass or catnip seeds to plant in a large clay pot filled with sterilized soil. Their feline friends will enjoy both. As an example, wheat grass seeds are large enough for small fingers to handle easily; they sprout in just a few days. The young gardener will have the double joy of watching and caring for emerging crops while also admiring the antics of cats who enjoy the fruits of these labors.

The real benefit of gardening with children, for all of us, is the information they gather from the flowers and plants, understanding how and where they grow and in which seasons. They will, with their inherent microscopic vision, begin to see the tiny creatures crawling about on all green things and to learn which flowers the birds like as future seeds and which ones butterflies choose as host plants.

In remembering the young fellow who befriended the traveling spider, you can see that there is a ripple effect children experience when they are encouraged in the ways of Nature. They see that it is a subtle tapestry of beauty with interwoven fascinations. This allows multilevel experiences stemming from their own curiosity and instinctive creativity.

Children continually surprise us with the ways in which they interpret Nature's gifts from the garden. Years ago, I was blessed with twin boys for next-door neighbors. They came over in the late afternoon almost every summer day just to look at the garden . . . or so they said. What they really wanted was a little clutch of flowers to take home to their mother . . . or so they said.

Their favorite "people" in the garden . . . so they said . . . were the snapdragons (*Antirrhinum*)—because you could make them talk—and naturally, snapdragons always went home with them. Grown men I know used those snapdragons as "soldiers" in their play battles when youngsters, forming them into battalions on a field of grass. Would that all battles could be fought so peacefully.

A decorated hat relaxing

The twins reminded me of my own sons' early interest in snapdragons, and I surmised that it was boy-like to enjoy most the blossoms that "did something," as if just being a full-blown fragrant, colorful, energetic flower wasn't enough.

Living in Maine as a young married woman, my summer gardening friend was the retired editor of a small-town New England newspaper. Karen White owned a black cat named Wendell Wilkie and a twenty-by-forty-foot rose garden bordered with perennials and mints of all sorts. She gardened at six o'clock in the morning wearing a pink nightie accessorized by a vintage editor's eyeshade in a deep faded green.

Karen, a brilliant woman whose home reflected both the past and present, had been retired from the newspaper business for five years when we met. She chiefly memorialized the past by stacking newspapers and magazines halfway up the walls, punctuated by more stacks of bright blue, two-pound coffee cans. The present was represented by open books on every remaining flat surface, and I knew that, with her sharp, inquiring mind, she was reading them all at once.

Some of those bright blue coffee cans served a noble purpose. All of the house's spaces that Karen used intimately—the table-top next to her typewriter, the breakfast table, the counter by the kitchen sink, the powder room, her bedside table, and the front hall table—were graced by coffee cans filled with antique roses cut from bushes inherited from her mother's garden.

Karen picked her flowers every morning putting them right into the blue cans, which were filled with warm water. It was a daily ritual for her, replacing faded blooms with fresh roses.

Humans weren't the only ones who enjoyed Karen's roses: Wendell Wilkie often sat by those coffee tins and from the corner of my eye—and on more than one occasion—I spied him surreptitiously inhaling their delectable essence!

Karen's front hall table was a genuine Gothic piece, with huge piano legs, the floor under its ten-foot length filled with a neat row of shoes—a supply to fit all occasions. I was taken back to Karen's hallway one day this summer. Coming up my own stairs as dawn broke, I saw pair after pair of my own work boots—some muddy, others pristine—lined up by the back door! Life is a repetition of patterns.

Remembering Karen White's gardens in Kittery, Maine, from forty years ago, I think we should all consider growing a few heirloom flowers. After all, to Karen, none of her flowers was a rarity, as we know them to be today. This situation has come about because of the predisposition of companies to hybridize their seeds and the tendency of growers to graft roses in order to "improve" them.

The most important thing to know about antique roses is that many varieties can live codependently with garden pests and survive under extreme climatic conditions. Whenever you visit family and friends, have a look around their gardens to see if old-fashioned iris, lilies, or other cherishables, including roses, might be growing in the corners. Ask for tubers, bulbs, seeds, and cuttings when they are available. A boon to northern gardeners, real heirloom roses are less apt to freeze, because they grow on their own root stock. Their very existence maintains a connection to the past, a timeline of soul nourishment, not unlike the shoe show bequest from a beloved friendship with an eccentric elderly lady who grew truly fabulous roses. Nature heals us.

Blossoms for a Summer Tea Party

Isn't it rewarding to know that our dreams are fulfilled in ways we never quite imagine? This summer I had the thrilling, albeit frantic, opportunity to have my family gathered here from the far corners, something that hadn't happened for several years. It was the perfect moment to plan a full-blown summer tea party

Veronica (Veronica 'Crater Lake Blue'), hot pink floribunda roses (Rosa chinensis 'Minima') blue scabiosa (Scabiosa caucasia 'Blue Perfection'), Queen Anne's lace (Daucus carota), pink larkspur (Consolida ambigua)

The children's old-fashioned summer tea party is centered by a small glass vase brimming with flowers from my garden. The linen napkins are tied with sprigs of ivy intertwined with floribunda roses and veronica. Herbal ice tea, rolled watercress sandwiches, and raisin scones invite the youngsters to tea.

Above: Rare pink Queen Anne's lace growing down in the meadow

Previous page: Overturned cups and smashed blackberries are indications of a successful tea party.

for my youngest grandchildren at the wonderful Clifton Country Inn, in Charlottesville, Virginia. We also shared "flower people" (as the children say) in a planned workshop nestled under huge old trees—a real challenge, considering the children's disparate ages.

Days before they arrived, I gathered the necessary accessories: immaculately starched napkins and tablecloths, teapots, cups and saucers, table and chairs, freshly ironed outfits for the little ones. I cut flowers for the tea table with the possibility in mind that the little guests could help with the actual flower ornamentations.

Having set the stage for their arrival, I felt the most enthusiastic member of the group, and so I waited expectantly for the drama to begin in the gardens of Clifton. Arrive they did, and the sudden pandemonium that accompanied them assured me that—where youngsters are concerned—everything would go according to plan . . . but not exactly mine!

For the commemorative photographs, one grandson refused to replace his black-and-red dragon-patterned socks with plain white ones . . . so we hid his feet under the tablecloth. Another demanded, theatrically and repeatedly, his mother's sunglasses. No one could be inveigled into showing the least bit of interest in the bounty offered on the table: berries, scones, jam, and watercress rollups!

Then, quite artistically, thirteen-month-old Bella smashed a giant couturier blackberry into the front of her flowered and starched dress. It was then that the party began to show some promise.

As if on cue, the youngsters dived into the delectable miniature tea sandwiches prepared for us by the Clifton chef, gulped iced herb tea served from a small glass pitcher, and turned over their cups of "cola tea" poured from a prim little teapot. Liveliness ruled: benches were toppled, strawberries were exchanged. We were watching a memory in the making.

After a quick change into more sensible clothes for the children, we set up an old wooden bench under a spreading and ancient tree to use as our worktable. The little ones began to inspect the buckets of flowers cut from my "wild" garden the evening before, wandering through them, not yet quite touching them. Watching their senses start to quicken was especially rewarding for this grandmother. The effect of the flowers was visibly more profound than that of the edibles set out on the tea table earlier. Smiles wreathed their faces, and concentration mixed itself with eagerness.

This was the first time most of the smaller ones had worked with flowers, and after tentative beginnings, they became totally immersed, producing great works of art. Two-year-old Kaci, not to be daunted at learning that short stems bend and break easily, figured out that she was able to stick larger, sturdier stems into her floral foam easily. Thus, her basket arrangement began to "grow" rapidly.

Cody from Colorado and Kody from Texas, three-and-a-half-year-old first cousins, became momentarily enamored of their small clippers and experimented with snipping stems. In the long run, flowers proved the greatest attraction to them. Neither stopped until their matching baskets of cosmos and goldenrod were abundantly and generously filled.

Martha and Claudia, gentle little ladies and neighbors, displayed serene behavior while their natural well-practiced artistry was given full-blown expression through a new art form.

My nine-year-old grandson Christopher, who had gardened and arranged during his visit the previous summer, went into production using past experience to expedite principles previously met and considered. He put his shortest flowers in the floral foam first, then proceeded with confidence to greater dimensions, finishing with an arrangement that stood about thirty inches tall!

We ended our satisfying day at four-thirty in the afternoon, corralling the children and packing up the cars. The children gave their remarkable flower arrangements to admirers among the inn's guests who had watched with enjoyment the growing creativity of happy beginners.

In retrospect, it was the best day of my life, and I hope it proves to be a landmark occasion for all my grandchildren as well.

Summer's Arrangement

One of the great joys of midsummer is fields of Queen Anne's lace, stretching sometimes as far as the eye can see. When there has been a good deal of rain, waves and waves of lace continue to bloom, with the plants seeming to grow taller each day.

With underlayers of black-eyed Susans flamboyantly cloaking the fields in richest yellows as a counterbalance to the superabundant Queen Anne's lace this summer, it seemed shameful to deny these two volunteers access to our summer arrangement. To use them extravagantly is to honor them. I try to notice what the wild is producing when planning flowers for a family dinner, party, or commercial event. In working with Nature you can use her largesse as the mainstay of your arrangements, adding chosen imported flowers if you wish.

In tune with this philosophy, I selected black-eyed Susans to be a reflective understory for our summer composition, along with an intended overprofusion of Queen Anne's lace — even some pink ones! An excellent general rule of thumb when using white flowers is to place yellows at their feet. Yellow has a freshening effect while making white seem even more white.

To begin our summer arrangement, I placed the black-eyed Susans in the oasis and added variegated hosta (*Hosta undulata*) and bunched lilyturf (*Liriope platyphylla*) leaves to help soften the edges of our old friend, the terra-cotta pot. It would have been more difficult, though not impossible, to add the shorter flowers later on.

Next, the actual dimensions—height and width—were determined by adding numbers of the longest stems of Queen Anne's lace, until the arrangement felt overly abundant. In wanting our summer arrangement to be an expression of the true exuberance of the season, I continued to fill all of the vacant spaces with more and more lace and lengthier Susans. At the very last, white phlox (*Phlox paniculata*) from the garden was added to give the center of the piece more visual weight.

As with our spring arrangement, the butter-yellow walls of Airlie House's sitting room served as background for the arrangement, acted as a filler, and added to the feeling of softness.

I understand that Queen Anne's lace is being used by some herbalists in resolving weight control and other issues, so check in with your herb practitioner to determine whether your summertime organic flower arrangement is edible. Those fields of lace have intrinsic value!

It is noteworthy that St. John's lace, almost a twin to our wild lace, is available practically year-round from the florist. It does not have the characteristic black dot in the center, cannot reproduce itself, is not invasive, and has a larger head than Queen Anne's lace, which is said to have come to this country long ago in the ballast of English sailing ships.

Looking Back on Summer

Summer days are longer, but there is much to do. We travel, perhaps entertain more, visit regularly with friends, neighbors, and family. Summer is the gardener's season, but with careful planning during the other months, we won't spend all the free summer hours working in our special garden places. We can enjoy both beauty and bounty, flowers and vegetables alike, even from afar.

In the summertime, I am reminded of gardening with my mother when I was young, and eating the vegetables from our

Queen Anne's lace (Daucus carota), black-eyed Susans (Rudbeckia hirta), variegated hosta (Hosta undulata), bunched lilyturf (Liriope platyphylla), and phlox (Phlox paniculata)

Many would dismiss the field flowers of our summer arrangement as mere weeds. They are indeed plentiful in most locations and once gathered can be lured into limitless representations of themselves, casual or elegant by choice.

A purple martin birdhouse, standing near the meadow, was my first spring purchase as the house neared completion. Because it was set on a pole too near the ground for martins, bluebirds instantly claimed it, returning to their condominium every March. At least three of the spaces are sequentially occupied throughout the summer for their nestlings.

own garden and those we bought from Old Charlie, who came to our house in a mule-drawn, umbrella-shaded wagon several times a week. His wagon was loaded with strawberries and melons, as well as all the wonderful summer vegetables—tomatoes, beans, and squash. Like all the children in the area, I looked forward to Charlie's visits; he was a sign of the season. To this day, summer means eating all the "Charlie foods." Savoring these vegetables and fruits just as they mature makes us a healthy part of the cycle of Nature.

Summer can be a capricious season as well. Here in Madison County this year, summer followed an exceptionally dry spring. Then, we were visited by a record-making flood and have ended the season with more than six weeks of drought and accompanying heat. The thirsty trees look almost sapless in some cases, and dogwood leaves will be turning early. Both we and the trees look forward to cooler autumn nights that lie just beyond a turn of the calendar's page. But this is all part of Nature's cycle. While summer is lush, autumn is pared down and winter spare. Spring returns with its glorious outburst of color and fragrance. Enjoy them all; their gifts are ours to savor.

As plants germinate in the Earth's night...
As herbs send forth shoots through the
atmosphere's power,
As fruits ripen through the strength of the sun...
So blooms the soul in the shrine of the heart...
So sprouts the spirit's strengths and the light of
the world
So matures the strength of man in the light of God.

——— Rudolf Steiner

Autumn

Autumn is the season of transition. Winters can "melt into spring," songwriters tell us, and with increasing frequency here in the Blue Ridge foothills, spring can suddenly reach into the peak of a summer's heat.

Autumn, however, is Nature's way of saying, "Pause, drink in my beauty." As the sky becomes wider, we become the colors of the sunset, absorbing the changing designs of clouds. We observe the day's softening light as dusk brings a sudden change in the temperature. At what other time of the year do colors become a deepening purple as the sun retreats and day gives way to evening?

The colors of day feel richer—sunrises sparkle, sunlit days enliven, and sunsets inspire—sustaining us. Autumn nightfall brings a hush so complete that crickets accompany only one another. There is a sense of nearing a completion. During evening walks, the air is suddenly filled with bats intent on their evening buffet, plummeting quickly as they collect flying insects in the growing darkness. They don't hesitate to dive quite close, a startling sensation compared with the classical dance of swallows that soared to the synchronized beat of unheard music in the earlier afternoons of summer.

With the coming of cooler air, dogs want to run off their energies, adding an after-dinner gambol in case there is adventure to be had since their five o'clock walk. They veer into the woods and return breathlessly to announce that deer are coming down for an evening's graze, maybe even the doe with her fawns. I anticipate a glance of these graceful creatures, but needn't worry about their coming up to the gardens. A summer's worth of authoritative barking leads the deer to believe

Honeysuckle (Locinera japonica), *sunflowers* (Helianthus annuus), *wild swamp grass, Joe Pye weed* (Eupatorium purpureum), *cockscomb* (Celosia argentea cristata)

By encouraging honeysuckle vines to tumble over the sides of a rusty watering can, I recreated the autumn sense of abundance and disarray. The flowers are crowded together and overrun by the rampant honeysuckle characteristic of my own fall garden.

Tulips (Tulipa), *blue fescue grass* (Festuca amethystina var. superba) *and lamb's ears* (Stachys byzantina)

In planting purple tulip bulbs alongside the steps and just above a framework of blue fescue and lamb's ears, I am counting on a "mood" piece for spring. The tulips' background is the stone of the house and the green of an oak-leafed hydrangea (H. quercifolia) *giving way to a foreground of blue-gray tones.*

The weather changes that come with autumn's especially cooler nights, encourage different kinds of growth. Many summer flowers take a deep breath and start off anew. Some varieties of heirloom roses bloom again! Zinnias and marigolds flourish, seeming more vibrant as the weather cools than they appeared while doing battle with August's heat. The rich deep red of maturing cockscomb (*Celosia argentea cristata*), rose pink sedum (*Sedum spectabile* 'Autumn Joy') and blue-purple hardy ageratum (*Ageratum houstonianum* 'Blue Bedder') brighten and grow more intense. The caryopteris (*Caryopteris x clandonensis* 'Bluebeard') offers us an option in the blue color field. We also have all colors and sizes of chrysanthemums along with spiky physostegia (*Physostegia virginiana*) and goldenrod (*Solidago odora*) to introduce into arrangements with the summer hangers-on. Some of the most glorious and accommodating plants for cutting bloom abundantly in autumn.

Early autumn compensates the gardener for the vagaries of summer weather. After the June flood waters receded and the inundated flowers, shrubs, and trees began their recuperation, the weather pattern here in the valley changed drastically. July brought the expected moisture, after which all precipitation stopped. By early September, we had had no rainfall for six weeks.

This summer's drought taught me how little water many flowers and plants really need if their roots are kept sufficiently cool with mulch. Many of the trees and shrubs did suffer greatly. I had to find a new approach to my policy of not watering established plantings. My concept of rules is that creatively breaking them is fun! I devised a selective system for drip irrigation. The heavy-duty nozzle of the hose has a flow regulator as well as an off/on dial. The effect is that a miniature trickle of water flows directly down into the main trunk of the selected tree, allowing one long drink. In actual time, the process takes from one to three hours for each tree or shrub. It is slow but thorough. So far the pump and water supply have supported the needs of my trees. Since learning that a great mature tree drinks more than two thousand gallons of water per day, my concern for the wooded land has grown. I wait anxiously to see what moisture the winter brings to counteract the effects of this year's drought.

Autumn is a great time of the year to try the unexpected in the garden. Visits to plant nurseries are a good place to start. At your favorite local nursery, consider hardy asters or Michaelmas daisies *(Aster)* instead of the usual chrysanthemums *(Chrysanthemum)*. These asters, which bloom in late September and October, range in height from twenty to forty inches at maturity. I have a five-year-old Aster 'Alma Potschke' that blooms brilliantly and spreads willingly. Aster 'Hella Lacey', 'Novae Angliae', 'Harrington's Pink', and 'Blue Lake' are all handsome specimens for the last hurrah of autumn.

Look closely at the October garden, and you'll begin to see colors differently; they become more muted. The riot of summer and early fall changes to deep blues, purples, and bronzes, colors that are palpable in feeling and royal in appearance.

In the old days, purple and red dyes were the most difficult to come by, so these rare colors were reserved for the clothes of royalty and lords of the manor, while the lesser folk wore those made mostly of undyed natural fibers. Many people today are again wearing those basic fibers by choice. Choice presents opportunity.

Think of the contrast evident between the so-called rich colors and the more muted earth shades; yet combining the two

A field of red fescue grass (Festuca rubra) in late afternoon light speaks of the fall colors to come.

Queen Anne's lace summer design. Fall is the time to be extravagant also with groupings of liriope's elongated lavender, granular-textured flower spikes, which are later followed by little black berries covering the stalk. The plants have multiple flower stems, which are the autumn equivalent of spring's grape hyacinths *(Muscari)*.

My particular garden favorites are striped eulalia grass *(Miscanthus sinensis variegatus)*, zebra grass *(Miscanthus sinensis zebrinus)*, ruby grass *(Rhynchelytrum repens)*, and ribbon grass *(Phalaris arundinacea pica)*. Both ribbon grass and zebra grass have variegations of white in their foliage, making them especially interesting as plant material. When you are wandering the fields and meadows of autumn, collect foxtail grass *(Alopecurus)*, wild oats *(Arrhenatherum)*, Johnson grass, and red fescue *(Festuca rubra)*.

Choice vines for fall picking—besides the indefatigable wild and garden honeysuckle *(Lonicera)*—are lablab or purple hyacinth bean *(Dolichos lablab)* for its purple pods, trumpet vines *(Campsis radicans)*, clematis *(Clematis)*, grape vines (arbor or wild), bittersweet *(Celastrus scandens)*, and wisteria *(Wisteria)*. These can all be cut in lengthy strands and twisted into wreaths or just hung to dry in their own convoluted shapes, as if they were still growing. The latter form is perfect for over-the-door garlanding.

There are magnificent evergreens right in our own gardens and backyards that are "must-haves" for fall and holiday use. Early to mid-September isn't a bit too soon to preserve magnolia *(Magnolia grandiflora)* and other evergreen branches in a glycerin solution. Cut the branches as long as six feet and trim two inches of bark off the cut ends. Remove damaged leaves and prune out excess small branches. Use one part glycerin to two parts boiling water, stir thoroughly, and place the trimmed stem ends of your evergreens into the mixture at a depth of four inches. The hot water encourages the branches to drink up the solution. If the greens absorb the solution completely, add more to the bucket.

Magnolia leaves usually take at least three to four weeks to turn a rich, dark brown. If beads of oil should appear on the leaves, the branches have been left in the solution a bit too long. Remove them and wipe both leaves and stem ends with a soft cloth or old toweling. The treated magnolia branches are best stored in a box in a cool, dry place. Your interestingly shaped preserved branches or tall grasses will be stunning line material in arrangements, placed first of all in the container to act as a field guide to your artistry. The preserved magnolia leaves also add interest to garlands when used individually.

In limiting our arrangements to flowers only, we overlook other possibilities from the grocery store. A wonderful vegetable to dry for fall and winter arrangements is the many-petaled artichoke. There are several ways to dry them, but my preference is what I call the "paper towel method." Roll up strips of plain white paper towel and push them down between each of the leaves; then, place the artichokes on trays on a cool, dark closet shelf for six weeks. Monitor the dampness carefully wherever they are stored, as artichokes will mildew easily, preferring to be in a very dry environment. To prepare them in advance for use in arrangements, you may push the sharp end of a green hyacinth stick into the artichoke's stem end before drying.

Flowers for an Autumn Hunt Ball

Two autumn traditions here in Virginia are fox hunting and steeple chasing, season-long events that culminate in sumptuous parties. One year, I was asked to prepare the table centerpieces for a steeplechase ball to be held at Montpelier, President James Madison's home near Orange, Virginia. The ball was to be a large event. Constructing the arrangements took four days. Two twelve-foot displays of dried flowers were designed in antique garden urns, one for the foyer of Montpelier, the other for the cocktail tent.

During the course of the preparations, the weather became cold and rainy, as it will in November. Four fellow workers and I spent one day arranging centerpieces in an elegant, frigid, centenarian barn whose horse stalls had been occupied in bygone days by champions. Our only light source came from bare bulbs dangling from the ceiling; worktables were sawhorses and planks. There was no heat to ward off the chill. Torrential rains made our world inhospitable on that autumn day. Feet and hands froze. Nevertheless, challenge and deadline were met. We countered both elements and surroundings with laughter and camaraderie, saving us from the perils of inevitable pneumonia.

Yet, with all the splendor of the arrangements we were creating and the companionship and resolve to persevere and triumph, my most vivid experience that week was the day I returned to Airlie Conference Center to "do" the weekly fresh flowers. When I arrived at Airlie, I felt quite spent, tired beyond exhaustion, still cold from the dampness of our day in the barn. Then, as masses of flowers arrived from the wholesaler, with their fullness of beauty and fragrance, I began to relax. The nourishment that only flowers provide started seeping into my soul. This was another experience of healing and renewal, placing me solidly in touch with my earth connection.

Photo to the left: Michaelmas daisies (Aster nova-belgii) Lilies (Lilium 'Monte Rosa'), bronze chrysanthemums (Chrysanthemum x morifolium), dried sunflower head (Helianthus annuus), goldenrod (Solidago odora), pincushion protea (Protea 'Pincushion'), Italian ruscus (Ruscus aculeatus), red onions, gourds, shiitake mushrooms, crabapples, fall crocus bulbs (Colchicum autumnale), and gloriosa lily (L. Rothchildiana).

Overleaf: Gathered from my woods and gardens: grapevines, hornet's nest, dried sunflower seedheads (Helianthus annuus), gourds, deer moss, pine cones, bird's nests, acorns, hickory nuts, chestnut shells, branches of crabapple, sassafras leaves, and a log washed up by the summer flood.

From my florist: purple lisianthus (Lisianthus Russellianus), purple Michaelmas daisies (Aster novi-belgii), spurge (Euphorbia polychroma), bronze and cremone chrysanthemums (C. x morifolium), orange lily (Lilium 'Montreaux') and peach lilies (Lilium 'Menton'), gloriosa lily (L. Rothchildiana), pincushion protea (Protea 'Pincushion'), and fall crocus bulbs (Colchicum autumnale).

From the grocery store: red onions, orange peppers, oyster mushrooms, shiitake mushrooms, red pears, and apples.

This year, fall was less spectacular than usual because of the drought, but the experience of it was nevertheless enriching.

Groundedness has a way of disappearing when we are overly scheduled or exhausted.

Organic Formality

The Thanksgiving arrangement was inspired by a weathered log I found after the June flood. Its long narrow shape is perfect for use as a centerpiece or, as I have situated it here, on a serving table in the dining room of Gayle and Stephen Bathon. I placed three green plastic florists' design bowls, each filled with a half block of well-soaked floral foam behind the log to steady it and act as flower holders. The fruits and collected elements from the "wild" were arranged first to act as the foundation for the composition, both visually and practically. They accomplished the important initial considerations: weighing down the log to prevent slippage and providing visual substance.

Because my goal was "organic formality," I wanted the final "look" to be richly colorful, and also to have the feel that it had just sprung from the forest floor. After the underpinnings were complete, I began working the flowers upward until the height of the tallest lily balanced well with the length of the "enchanted" log. Balance is in the eye of the beholder and has nothing to do, so far as I am concerned, with actual measurements. Some of the lilies have their stamens removed, others do not. There is a reason. At the last minute I needed replacements and Village Flowers in Warrenton, Virginia, came to my rescue. In conditioning lilies, they always remove the stamen to promote longevity.

There is no question that a work replete with as many details as this one must be thought out in advance, the flowers ordered, and collectibles gathered. However, once the numerous parts and pieces are gathered in a chosen place, the fun begins. Practicality, born of experience, told me where to begin. I pass this information on to those who wish to make playmates of logs and fungi. The beginning is the adventure, the process is the joy, and the finishing is the sense of ultimate completion, until the next beginning.

An Often-Forgotten Taste Treat

During the autumn months, roadsides, ill-tended gardens, and woodland borders are rich with the brilliant gold of Jerusalem artichokes (*Helianthus tuberosus*). The majesty of their masses is unequaled, and just observing these sunflowers in their super-abundance brings a special lightness to our being.

While native Americans used them as a remedy for rheumatism, there's another way to benefit from these invasive but magnificent growers. After frost and throughout the winter, dig their tubers (they keep better left in the ground rather than stored in basements) to eat raw or cooked! My personal preference is to enjoy their raw state. They have a crunch much like water chestnuts. For a tasty addition to the autumn dinner table, simply peel and steam them for about seven minutes, then prepare them as you would mashed potatoes or turnips.

Jerusalem artichokes also make an excellent pickled relish for cold meats:

Celebrating the Season

Flower shops are engaging. Their fragrance and color captivate the senses. I enter such special places as if bewitched, especially the ones with buckets of flowers beckoning from the sidewalk.

Autumn is a perfect time to rediscover these local shops, as well as the aforementioned plant nurseries. Notice the yellows, pinks, blues, lavenders, and purples of fall-blooming asters and luxuriantly blooming hardy hibiscus (*Hibiscus moscheutos*) found in whites, pinks, and purples. The hibiscus provide a bonus later on. Their pods grow in curious, medium-sized bunches and can be used in dried arrangements. When cut, the flower blooms themselves only hold well if placed immediately in the refrigerator to harden off. They will then last long enough to brighten a dinner party, wilting as the clock strikes twelve!

Another reason to frequent flower and garden shops at this time of year is to simply learn from the many ideas that germinate in such surroundings. After asking in several of my favorite garden shops why the chrysanthemums that I knew as a child were unavailable, I found that there are several wholesalers who grow the unusual, old-fashioned varieties. My plan is to be in touch with them in the hope that they sell fewer than a truckload per order.

From my experience, proprietors of these stores will be more than happy to speak to your needs, searching and recommending, as in the case of my old-fashioned mums. Staying

*A container built of recycled material
is the vehicle for a quick mix of multi-
headed, easily reseeding garden celosia and
zebra grass. I lined it with sheet
moss (available from your florist) inside
of which I put a glass vase. The mechanics
consist of one block of floral foam cut to
fit into the vase in a vertical fashion.
I customarily soak sheet moss in water
(squeezing it out carefully) whenever I
add it to arrangements. In this instance,
however, it was imperative to keep it dry
as the piece was going directly onto
a table at Airlie House.*

curious in order to run down special seasonal varieties for your
garden ultimately enhances future flower compositions.

Information-gathering in flower shops, especially in the fall,
shows us the newest trends in the design world: unusual color
combinations and special containers freshly on the market.
What a perfect environment in which to meet unknown flowers
and decide how to adapt them—along with ideas—to your personal lifestyle.

While thinking of autumn shapes and colors, one seasonal
element clearly cannot be overlooked. Giant leaves emerge
mysteriously from a trusted flower bed, vines grow, and huge
orange blossoms appear immediately on their heels. A surprise
pumpkin vine, which seems nonthreatening at first, takes over
the entire bed. One such unexpected visitor is the source of
numerous stories this fall.

*Bittersweet (Celastrus scandens),
Chinese bamboo, chrysanthemums
(Chrysanthemum 'Garnet King' and
C. 'Cremone'), American beautyberry
(Callicarpa americana), cockscomb
(Celosia argentea cristata),
goldenrod (Solidago annuus)*

*The fall arrangement, done in our
terra-cotta pot, incorporates dried and
fresh materials. I used swirls of bittersweet
vines and flower heads of zebra grass to
establish the outside perimeter of the
finished piece. The grasses and Chinese
bamboo give drama and determine the
scale of the piece.*

*Grasses provide strong verticality to
offset the visual weight of darker garnet
king chrysanthemums, cremone
chrysanthemums, and beautyberries
grouped at the center. Adding golden
cockscomb and goldenrod plays up the yellow "eye" of the cremone. Because I used
both dried and fresh materials in this
piece, it is a natural holdover for the
winter months. As the chrysanthemums
die, they may be cut off (as close to the
floral foam as possible) and replaced with
other materials such as hydrangeas, okra,
stalks of cotton or fresh flowers. If it is
necessary to remove water from the
container, do so with a turkey baster.*

markings. In those later years, even though her vision and hearing were not as discerning as in her youth, Delilah wouldn't hesitate to take an independent stroll in the late afternoon. It became a common sight, though one to which I never became accustomed, to see a skunk sharing her walk, a respectful distance of maybe twenty feet between them. She didn't discriminate, always preferring companionship during a country ramble.

Delilah was a friend of so many years that she will be impossible to replace. I have not yet found a sufficiently adventuresome "dog person" to be new companion-in-residence. Other dogs visit, and their status is just that: visitors only.

Leaving Autumn Behind Us

Autumn is a season of contradictions—we see around us the fading of summer's grandeur, all the while experiencing a burst of renewal before the onset of winter's quiescence.

The sight of exuberant color as leaves change; the sound of crickets in the thickening dusk; the taste of crunchy apples and freshly pressed cider; the cooler, crisper air all stimulate us. Gardens and insect or animal visitors combine with these sensations to present a feast of delight, served up by Nature herself.

Things we plant in our gardens at this season will thrive, benefiting from the opportunity to establish serious roots over the coming winter months. The rewarding hours spent digging now content us to bide time over the winter, knowing that the fruits of autumn labors will thrill with spring's return engagement.

Perhaps it is necessary for us, as the days shorten, to take the time to savor the world around us, to connect with the earth.

*Eternal life is only awareness. Understanding that everything
participates in circles of return. That everyone will be transfigured and reborn. Even a stone will become earth, in which a tree
will bear fruit to be eaten by a child, which will become the
twinkle of an eye. Everything will change. And the Holy One
will meet everything backstage, in between performances. He will
answer all questions and show us all of eternity from one end to
the other.*

—Lawrence Kushner

WINTER

When the colors of Nature take a much-needed vacation, leaves decorate our lives differently. They go underfoot to hide familiar landmarks, jump into the water to go on float trips, and assemble themselves obligingly to insulate perennial beds from the frost.

When decorating trees and shrubs, they act as cushions, absorbing sound. In falling away they allow audible reverberations of the valley to become intensified. The sounds are magnified as they travel through the crisp, cold air of winter. The loudspeaker snapping of a branch breaking under the weight of snow or a tree falling in the forest seems as close as the crackling log in the fire.

Geese from the nearby nature preserve, out for a stretch, converse overhead in voices so precise that I feel included in the gossip. It was obvious early on that the house occupies space in a bird flyway, which was one of the determining factors for feeder locations. The tall, spindly maple planted in the middle of the birds' path serves as lookout station during lineups at the feeders. The dinner music engendered by this now less colorful, not so vociferous band begins and ends winter days with cheer.

Ice castles crunch underfoot. We've all seen the heavings of frozen water-soaked soil. Children want to know of the unseen: Who is pushing these little castles upward from their earlier incarnation as muddy rain-soaked earth? Some castles wear towers of shaggy green moss, others have acorn caps posing as frosty turrets, the whole surrounded by crisp, frost-whitened leaves.

Plant life growing through frozen edges of streams takes on a new demeanor. Ice flowers intermingle with rocks made

Winter vista of the meadow:
New patterns in the winter valley
are created by floodwaters.

colorful by contrastingly dead grasses. Together they decorate an otherwise monochromatic streambed. Winter's delicate frosty formations of crystalline lace cover seedpods that glisten in an early morning's sun.

These fragile paintings, which melt as temperatures rise, are completely obliterated during a deep snowfall. Snow encourages quietude, fills in crevices, facilitates shapeliness. Its blanketing rounds the blunt edges of things, softening. Unfamiliar undulations beckon to us: "Come explore the changed landscape," they say. These shapes, like the round hay bales of summer, bring sensuousness to the land.

Continuing snow provides quietude for the earth and the realization that one of the most deafening sounds of winter is silent snowfall. In what T. S. Eliot calls "lucid stillness," we hear the resonance of the universe.

In these moments, the falling ax of a neighbor who is splitting logs for his woodstove moves out of itself into the rhythm of belonging. Its echoes vibrate to form new patterns in the winter valley.

Winter in the Blue Ridge

The Blue Ridge Mountains were long ago given the name descriptive of the ever-present haze that envelops them. They are some of the oldest mountains in the world and, to me, the most inviting. Their foothills mimic their larger topography. Few who come to the Blue Ridge fail to fall in love with them.

These mountains and foothills form the backdrop for most of my visual perceptions. They frame the main perennial gardens and offer vistas for day or night dreaming. Their outline is visible at all times, unless shrouded in fog.

When I turn my back to the Blue Ridge and walk in the surrounding forest, I am in a quieter place. Footfalls are an event and animal tracks are easy to follow. Climbing, I cut across the mountainside following deer paths.

There is much to see. The winter bare bones of the forest are descriptions of changes that occurred in the preceding seasons. This year, rampaging June waters rearranged some of my favorite places. The antiquated swinging grapevine now lies on the ground, part of a new landscape; twisted and gnarled like a giant necklace, it wears boulders as its jewels.

Another site that was perceptibly altered by the flood is an area that I call the "tea room." This cozy spot for lunches on the go was "furnished" by a rectangular stone table surrounded by smaller boulder benches. The main stone lies on its side, no longer able to accommodate picnic baskets. My little room is unrecognizable, but winter explorations provide the opportunity to find new "dining-out" facilities for spring and summer workshops.

Untouched by Nature's angry hand, the laurel grove stands elegantly aloof. A feeding station for deer that delight in nibbling the tips of the mountain laurel (*Kalmia latifolia*) when vegetation becomes scarce, the great bushes have never bloomed during my tenure here. It is clear that the grove is also winter bedroom to deer. Its evergreen canopy gives protection from the elements. Because it is on a slope, the soil drains quickly, making the campsite cozier.

Woodpiles, stacked in preparation for cold nights ahead, give a different spatial quality to narrow stretches of porch. This winter's wood is primarily the abundant and fast-burning poplar. It blazes brilliantly and dies young.

When building the chimneys, the stonemason installed special vents that draw air from the outside, making all the fireplaces very efficient at their main job—warming the house.

These fireplaces get a thorough workout, especially when they serve as cookstoves during power outages. Ritual marshmallow toasting during the visits of teenage grandchildren is a long-standing tradition. We gather round the hearth and cook "S'mores." I learned to love them in my young summertime years at camp. To make one "S'more," simply sandwich four small squares of a chocolate bar and one toasted marshmallow between two graham crackers. It wouldn't be a real winter without serving them to favorite people while reminiscing about times gone by.

Marshmallowy treats notwithstanding, my preference for dining is to eat in the great outdoors; so I have no dining room. Each of the three porches has a table and chairs, and many a winter day will find me lunching with the sun, comfortable in turtleneck and jacket.

To me, eating outdoors is more of an event than the most elegant of indoor repasts. It is a true celebration. When the house was under construction, one rock became a favorite viewing spot, so I naturally served lunches there. It was only large enough to act as a small table, and the earth was my chair. The rock, now dwarfed by driveway, daylilies, and mulch pile, seemed larger then.

Below: Winter pokeweed berries (Phytolaca americana) *with oakleaf hydrangea* (Hydrangea quercifolia).

Potted herbs are an elegant gift, and I delight in offering them to friends as early messengers of the springtime that is soon to come. Blooming colorfully, it is as if the gardens had thought to come inside to escape from midwinter cold. I plant my gifts in eight- or ten-inch "wide-mouthed" bulb pots, which are perfect for several layers of progressive spring bloom. After placing a layer of gravel or clay pot shards at the bottom of a flower pot, add several inches of potting soil. Next, place four to six daffodil or tulip bulbs in the pot, add more soil, then a layer of miniature daffodils, more soil, and a final layer of grape hyacinths. The idea is to put the largest bulbs at the deepest level in the flower pots. Helpful planting charts are readily available in garden centers. The finished products may be placed in the refrigerator or "heeled into" the garden (meaning either buried in the ground or covered deeply with mulch). Twelve to thirteen weeks is an appropriate chill time, after which they may migrate either to your living room or to that of a friend.

I include saucers with containers of gift bulbs and seal the saucers' bottoms carefully with clear shellac. Gluing a piece of felt over the shellac protects tabletops so the pots are instantly usable indoors, being both scratch- and leak-proofed.

There is a corner of the garden for "heeling in" my own spring bulbs. They ususally come indoors in February and begin to bloom within about a month of getting their feet warm. The gift bulbs go into the refrigerator in October where the constant cool temperature is more dependable. Of course, the shelf space previously claimed by vegetables diminishes. Gardeners admit it—priorities change.

Food for Winter Thoughts

The first snow of the season always causes a bird flurry. The no-longer-gold finches cling to feeders, loudly debating who should claim the few sunflower seeds left adhering to nearly faded blooms. They become quite quarrelsome; gone is their soaring devil-may-care attitude of summer. Now they are distinctly territorial, and I keep wondering if birds might be encouraged to sign peace treaties!

As fall becomes winter and the natural foods from which to choose are rare, I can understand how the "groceries" living in the Medicine Wheel feeders are in high demand. It is a gladsome thing to find throngs gathered at mealtimes.

As for the local humans, wintertime and soup are synonymous words. The bigger the pot, the better. Freezing soup in small portions, so that its nourishment is available on a moment's notice, is the only way to go when faced with the

Potted paperwhite narcissus with a fragrant Osage orange ready for holiday giving. Fruits of the Osage orange (Maclura pomifera) tree were brought indoors for winter fragrance during Colonial days.

sense of ease. We've all experienced it. When power is restored and the "outside world" is back in working order, we are sad that our silence has been shattered.

This year, I have promised myself a few days of self-imposed winter isolation, storm or no storm, the intent being to emphasize the liberty of leisure. During my retreat, I will probably spend the time meditating and absorbing soul/mind/body nourishment from books, doing body-strengthening exercises, taking unhurried walks in winter fields (as opposed to climbing the mountainside), and eating mostly vegetables and fruits along with products made of spelt flour. Included will be herbal teas and lengthy warm-water body soaks with Masada salts from the Dead Sea. I heartily recommend reclusive interludes whenever you can allot the time from a hurried life. It's not easy to find seclusion, but it is worth it.

Another antidote to the stress of day-to-day life is a recipe almost nine-hundred-years old. It comes from Hildegard of Bingen, a twelfth-century German mystic. Quenched wine, an ancient nerve tonic, can effectively supplement the time we spend only with ourselves.

You might also wish to acquaint yourself with Hildegard's writings. She was a brilliant, multidimensional woman of her time whose writings have relevance for us today.

Recipe for Quenched Wine

Using a stainless steel pan, heat one glass of the best wine you have, either red or white, to the boiling point. (The alcohol in the wine will be reduced to less than two percent as a result of the boiling.) When the wine comes to a full boil, add, in one motion, one-half glass of cold water, the best you have available. Pour into a glass and sip.

A Special Birthday Gift

My second birthday at Naramata was special. I had spent months organizing the garden spaces. Life had now developed its own routine of daily, weekly, and monthly chores and activities. Taking a day off to celebrate, I decided to look in on the source of my mountain stream. It is a place whose energies provide equanimity. A month had gone by since my last visit there, and I wanted to see the mosses and little ferns down by the water's edge, thriving still in cooler weather.

That magical place held a surprise—an immense piece of white quartz. It sat right at the mouth of the spring! A large

Iced oak leaf

quartz rock is a rarity around Naramata, the usual ones being fist-sized. I gave the quartz a loving nudge with my foot to confirm its weight. It didn't budge. Sure this was a birthday gift, I determined to transport it somehow to my bathroom. A perfect place for its triangular shape was the edge of the gray-tiled bathtub.

It wasn't until I got back to the house that I started having doubts, so I had a long think about whether my new "Bathing Rock" should live inside or if it were better left alone. All the answers were: "Yes, bring it home!" Now the question to be answered was: "How?"

The next day, an old friend came to visit, and the appearance of her blue-jeaned self gave me the answer. She had no idea that her attire had determined a possible after-lunch agenda. Discussing the possibilities, we hauled out the heavy-duty wheelbarrow and headed for the stream. Slipping up the mossy embankment, wrestling the Bathing Rock into the wheelbarrow, we listened to its noisy clamoring against the bottom of the wheelbarrow all the way home.

Another first, we rolled the wheelbarrow up outside steps and through the bathroom door. Carefully placed on the tub's edge—its new living quarters—the quartz is a monumental gift from the land.

Remedies

Acceptance of flower essences, herbal tinctures, and homeopathic remedies as "medicine" brings us closer to nature. When we employ her gifts to mend body, mind, and spirit we also achieve a greater connectedness to our universe. Coming into what is called balance and harmony allows openness to new possibilities, from which our visions and lives expand.

Certified herbalists conduct workshops for teaching the preparation of tinctures, infusions, and decoctions. Caution is recommended as some herbs can be toxic.

Flower essences nourish the emotions. Taken in the form of tinctures, they can be purchased in health food stores.

Homeopathic remedies are made from animal, vegetable, and mineral sources. The theory which guides their use is the Law of Similars which is older than Hippocrates and decrees that "like heals like." These remedies treat the energy of the body, rather than the mass. The homeopathic physician prescribes small white tablets or liquids which contain minute amounts of natural substances intended to heal particular symptoms in the patient.

Family doorknocker wreathed
for Christmas

My own interest in the world of natural remedies began spontaneously. I clearly remember a time about twenty-five years ago when, in the name of eradicating dandelions from the lawn, my daylilies also disappeared. After that experience, herbicides were forever banned from my life. That single event set me wondering also about other man-made aids to "civilization." What about pesticides, certain cleaning products, and medicines we all accepted as normal adjuncts to life?

Today, after years of study and exploration, I am gaining the confidence to dig up dandelion roots for making my own tinctures. Attending educational seminars that teach about the healing properties of herbs and homeopathic remedies has become a way of life.

This approach includes animal care. Fig Newton visits the veterinarian for rabies shots. Otherwise, she receives homeopathic remedies. To discourage fleas, a special coat conditioner containing minute amounts of sulphur is added to her food. I remember my mother dusting the insides of her shoes with sulfur when she gardened. This discouraged ticks and chiggers. Modern-day hikers use the same trick, so no wonder it is a help to our four-legged loyalists.

For years, Delilah, my poodle friend, was terrified of thunderstorms. After I learned to treat her fear homeopathically, she stopped her habit of taking refuge in the bathtub when thunderstorms threatened. She began to merely notice storms, rather than react fearfully. With such positive results in animals, imagine the potential for humans.

There are many sources for over-the-counter homeopathic, herbal, and flower remedies. Before delving into them, however, I recommend research and training. There are many books on these subjects and it isn't hard to find licensed doctors and practitioners to help in your search for another way. The more your knowledge grows in these fields, the more you will understand the part intuition plays. Remedies, teas, and tinctures open a whole new lifestyle to us.

For example, several overlooked facts are vital to the success of healing with homeopathic medicines. It is important to avoid aromatics, such as wintergreen, camphor, eucalyptus, and menthol. Drinking coffee also interferes with homeopathic action. Homeopathics (liquid or pellet form) must be vigorously shaken before use to activate their potency. Homeopathic dosages are energy.

Herbal teas fit perfectly into a winter way of life. We talked of sipping them in front of a fire, after a long, snowy walk. They can also be an excellent introduction to the use of herbal tinctures and flower remedies for healing. When you begin your own research, you will discover the efficacy of many so-called common weeds, and perhaps decide to encourage them to grow on your own land.

Herbal teas and tonics bring nutritional nourishment to the whole body. They are especially effective in relieving stress during times of crisis because they enable the body to regain the homeostasis, or physiological equilibrium, that it naturally seeks. Flower remedies work through the emotional system to heal the body. Healthy emotions produce healthy bodies.

Herbs can enliven your home environment, too. Collect both lavender (*Lavandula*) and rosemary (*Rosmarinus officinalis*) to hang in closets or place between folded linens. They may be fresh or dried and are attractive tied in bunches about eight inches in length. Rosemary, planted close to the foundation for winter protection, grows well in my garden, but has never flowered. I compensate by growing several varieties of lavender that can be coaxed into blooming twice (once in June, again in September), if I persist in trimming the June flowers for use in bunches. I take a spool of baling twine to the garden with me and tie the sprigs together as I cut. Turned into thoughtful presents by tying bows of pretty ribbon around them, they add individuality to your gift-wrapping efforts.

Herbal oils for the bath are almost immediately gratifying to make. Pack lavender blossoms tightly into a small sterilized bottle, then fill it to the top with a good grade of olive oil. Seal tightly and place the bottle in both sun and moonlight for three to six weeks, preferably for two full moon cycles before actual use. Add several luxurious drops to your bath water.

For cosmetic purposes, a walk through your health food store shows you what is available in the marketplace. I prefer organically grown herbs in both beauty products and foodstuffs. Explore possibilities to discover your own favorites.

Winter Creativity . . . and Elegance

When my grandsons were children, we created the family's holiday centerpiece together. They collected the "ingredients" for our Thanksgiving tables as they walked home from school: grasses and precious found objects like rocks, twigs, attractively-shaped tree branches, and dried wild mushrooms. If they had no treasures, we went off to the grocery store and each one chose fruits or vegetables to include in their design. To our Christmas arrangement, which was often as spontaneous as the one pictured here, we added colorful elves which were constructed of pipe cleaners then dressed in felt doublets and peaked caps. Each came with long, lively personal histories fresh from the creative minds of the boys. It is always of my grandsons that I think when planning holiday table designs. Their youthful joy is reflected in the decorations we work on together for family gatherings.

By seasonal necessity, winter workshops take on a different

A winter overcoat for Naramata grasses

Boxwood (Buxus sempervirens), *poinsettias* (Euphorbia pulcherrima), *logs, lichen, hornets' nests and magnolia branch tips* (Magnolia grandiflora)

Teenage grandsons and their friends created this holiday table decoration. Some poinsettias were "bagged," others cut with stem ends burned to seal them. The project began with a twisted log found after the great summer flood. Three green florist's design bowls filled with floral foam steady the log and hold flowers and greens. The young people added magnolia, boxwood, and other greens, along with poinsettias. They started by teasing one another and ended up admiring a "community effort!"

tone. Winter gives us invigorating walks in the woods. We find heretofore unnoticed natural elements to include in arrangements and tablescapes, whose main flowering ingredients now come from the florist shop. Working indoors with sparer elements of design, it becomes easy to examine and concentrate on just how our creativity originates.

Over the years, I have found that reason is essential in ultimately producing and maintaining a creative lifestyle. Mechanical breakdowns or dysfunctions—broken doorsteps, keys that don't unlock, furnaces that don't heat—create irritability and make it harder to reach into our centers and maintain a balanced way of being. By observing and understanding the outside influences that tend to block creativity, it is possible to give yourself a "jump start" for finding imaginative solutions.

My term for this approach is "cultivated creativity." We can more easily enrich our lives with beautifully ordered and dedicated living through awareness of these negative influences. Essentially, the greatest thing disorder might produce is confusion and the urge to run away, while creativity feeds on more creativity, inculcating vitality with a sense of personal fulfillment.

According to a legend in Costa Rica, a blossom of ageratum (*Ageratum*) carried in your wallet will ensure that your needs will always be met. Supposedly you must take care to pick the flower from the field of an already wealthy person! The gist of this legend made me question the value of wealth. It is, after all, the promise to ourselves to create plenty in all aspects of our lives, beginning with love. Flowers, as an example, are an enabling factor in caring about ourselves and others—both those for whom we have affection and those we'll never meet. Wealth, to me, is the wisdom to fill our lives with the beauty and joy of abundance, coupled with a desire to share this fortune.

We have all had the experience of arranging flowers for a less-than-perfect spot or planting seeds where they simply won't grow. When things don't work, they give us know-how for the next attempt. We change our container, find taller, shorter, or more dramatic flowers. We plant seeds under different soil conditions. We create differently based on past experience; we make our own abundance.

My teenage grandson and his friends "help" me carry wreath-making grapevines found in the woods to our winter workshop.

Assembling the grapevine into a huge wreath for Naramata's back porch takes a strong back.

Finding our own way unleashes the productivity inherent in each of us. Expressed creativity provides wealth to the spirit in the form of nourishment and elegance. Elegance is something we all recognize when we see it; it is a possibility everywhere and in everything. It is the gait of a fine and curious horse; it is the demeanor and energy of a proud and intelligent dog. It is reflected in the burst of a dandelion from the earth, the swaying of a lily in gentle breezes, a woodside border of dogwood trees in midspring, a field of yellow buttercups, blue chicory, or Queen Anne's lace; it is a strand of favorite pearls.

We all respond to elegance; we want it for ourselves and, becoming more aware, we can each produce it in our lives. We arrange articles in our homes with care; we add violet, dandelion, or mustard blossoms to our salads in the spring; we place one flower in a simple vase on the dinner table. Children respond to elegance and adults are nurtured by all its forms. Simple but not plain, it is the responsive color in the comfortable place. It is simply elegant.

A Holiday Topiary Design

This growing topiary was created in our now familiar terra-cotta pot. I built the tree out of three presoaked pieces of floral foam: two stacked designer blocks topped by a regular sized brick. They are held together with eighteen-inch hyacinth sticks pushed through all three blocks. I shaped the foam by cutting off square sides with my knife, then secured the blocks with two strips of davey tape crossing each other in an x at the top and extending over the pot sides. Next I placed a circle of tape around the upper edge of the pot, covering the four ends of tape. The entire form was covered with poultry wire which I also taped to the pot with davey tape. (Note: If the pot gets wet, let it dry before attaching tape.)

Bunches of tiny dried red peppers, rose hips picked in the fall, Foster holly, boxwood, magnolia branch tips, and red cedar were stuck directly into the wet floral foam along with cut branches of azalea (from greenhouse plants). After inserting the root balls of cyclamen plants into plastic freezer bags, I attached the bags to the poultry wire frame using taped wires, thus insuring that the cyclamen will not be overwatered. Hand-painted angels and wired ribbon (both attached to shortened hyacinth sticks) were the final touch.

A construction of this sort is an excellent project in which to include children.

This topiary requires a "shower bath" twice a week because the floral foam is not fixed to "wick" water. A practical solution is to place the topiary in a four-inch deep roasting pan, removing any perishable decorations such as angels and ribbon, and water from above with either a small watering can or the hose attachment of your kitchen sink. Drain thoroughly before placing it in the plastic saucer of "look alike" terra-cotta. (The plastic is used for safety's sake.) Kept in a relatively cool room, your topiary should have a longevity of two to three weeks.

Poinsettias being the popular mainstay of Christmas arrangements, it is helpful if they last for several weeks. A sure way to keep small poinsettias fresh for the entire holiday season without having to water them again is the following method I learned working with the Altar Guild of the National Cathedral in Washington, D.C. I also used this method for the cyclamen plants included in the Christmas topiary.

Hybrid poinsettia (Euphorbia pulcherrima *'Monet'*)

Using a one-quart size plastic freezer bag and twist-ties, follow this procedure for each plant:

1. Place four-inch pots of poinsettias in about six inches of water in the kitchen sink and let them soak for one hour. Drain the pots overnight.

2. Inverting the pot in your hand and tapping the bottom, carefully remove plant and soil from the container.

3. Squeeze the ball of dirt to remove excess water.

4. Place ball in the plastic freezer bag, cutting off excess bag length if necessary so that you have just enough plastic left around the stem of the poinsettia to secure the bag tightly with a twist-tie. (Do not use zippered baggies.)

5. Tuck the plant down into your arrangement, hiding the plastic bag with greens or mosses. In my experience, the so-called "bagged plants" last far longer than the individually cut poinsettia flowers.

The First Naramata Christmas

Walking a plank is a phrase we would expect to hear from pirates. They're not the words we usually associate with entering someone's front door. But "walking the plank" became the standard way to enter my house in its building stage.

Because I moved into the house during actual construction, the usual amenities, such as a front porch, were not yet in place. A twelve-foot-long board provided access to the double front doors. Not frequently intimidated by heights, the fourteen-foot drop below struck terror in my heart as I first crossed the narrow span carrying bags of groceries. Delilah was equally apprehensive. The most immediate way of urging her to cross was the "old rat in the maze" formula of dinner at the end of the runway. Even after the builders had long departed, if she were really hungry, Delilah would sometimes check at the red front doors just in case I had misplaced her dinner plate!

In actuality, entering the house in so dramatic a fashion became quite commonplace, even for guests. When the aggregate porch was finally poured and cured, it seemed an accommodation added for sissies.

My living accommodations during most of the building process were the only habitable area in a still-evolving shell—the everything room. This space, now called the guest bedroom, served as bedroom, office, and dining room and was connected to a graceless bathroom equipped with only Jacuzzi bathtub and "water closet." In learning new habits, such practices as bending over the side of the tub to brush my teeth began to seem per-

Red cedar (Juniperus virginiana), *Foster holly* (Ilex x attenuata 'Fosteri'), *boxwood* (Buxus sempervirens), *magnolia branch tips* (Magnolia grandiflora), *dried red peppers, rose hips, azalea* (Rhododendron 'Champagne'), *and miniature cyclamen* (Cyclamen cyprium)

Opposite: Our Christmas tree bouquet, placed on a front hall table, celebrates the season by welcoming guests with glad spirit. Constructed by family members as a holiday project, it can also replace a traditional tree in the closer spaces of a house or city apartment.

fectly normal. I, like Delilah and Fig, found myself accustomed to a different lifestyle.

As the holiday approached, it seemed that my first Christmas in such unvarnished surroundings would be bleak. Being determined to celebrate, I willfully carried a tree over the elongated threshold. Adorned with spirals of tiny gold stars, it was installed in the everything room.

Gold stars were also thumbtacked to the spackled gray drywall in the bath. Celebration is all in the eye of the beholder, and these stars echoed the diamond-studded skies just outside bedroom doors. Since coordinating decor with surrounding amenities has always been a point of focus for me, this particular star struck holiday was notable!

For a Holiday Mantel

For a Christmas mantel design, I added poinsettias to a previously assembled grouping of winter greens collected from woods and garden. Common Virginia pine, whose trailing

Poinsettias (Euphorbia pulcherrima *'Angelica' and 'Angelica White'*), *native pine* (Pinus virginiana), *magnolia* (Magnolia grandiflora), *and other greens collected from woods and garden*

branches grow in a tenuous way, forms the framework of the piece, with shiny magnolia leaves providing animation and weight, also acting as filler.

I inserted the lower pine branches into the floral foam at an upward angle to give the appearance of being still attached to their tree. They give a naturalistic sense to the completed piece. Wanting the added poinsettias to be lengthy, I cut, then burned their stem ends until I no longer heard a sizzling sound, placing shorter ones directly into the arrangement. Remaining stems were inserted into filled water tubes attached with davey tape to green bamboo garden stakes. The extra length gave needed height to poinsettia branches, whose parent plant, a nursery grown poinsettia, was thrown away after being denuded.

I make the effort, when looking for line material, to visualize how it will be used, instead of just collecting helter-skelter. My habit is to cut the intended central branch first. I lay it on the ground and add each succeeding green to the imaginary structure which now lies prone at my feet. The same procedure is repeated with magnolia branches. Whenever I cut from shrubs or trees, I am consciously pruning, which makes quick work of two jobs. Be sure to keep your woody garden growth in good health by consulting an authoritative guide on winter pruning procedures.

Finishing touches for the mantel arrangement

Endings and New Beginnings

December is an excellent month. The garden has been put to bed and the house becomes the center of interest. Splendid amaryllis buds celebrate by bursting open, as the second round of Christmas cactus sing in tune with perfumed narcissus bulbs grown in containers filled with stones or gravel.

Some of our time is hectic, planning and executing family celebrations. Those hours are balanced by contemplative ones spent wrapping presents, baking cookies, and writing holiday notes to friends. All are heartfelt endeavors giving stimulus to our expressive selves. This is the time of the year we loose the reins, making special ornaments and decorations with children, and recognizing long-established family rituals as priorities. The trick for me is not getting lost in the uproar, keeping life force attuned rather than letting the mind assume leadership.

Now on my Virginia hillside in late January's new year, the house is shrouded in phantom-like swirls, frenzied snow that is whipped around its corners by twenty-five-mile-an-hour winds. I stand looking down on a road that I cannot see, the lower third of my body enveloped by snow that underlies the depleted bird feeders. The wintering birds and I are being challenged by

Wedding ribbon with a new twist

a blizzard that will soon be a memory as their Medicine Wheel sanctuary is once again alive with songs, merriment, and fragrance.

Flames lap the edges of well-dried logs cut from the land last year. My dreams become immersed in seed catalogs as I envision the vibrant hues of spring gardens to come.

Now is the time to pause and think both prudently and whimsically about how to make a reality of carefully laid plans, how to bring about garden environments in which to work and thrive. The perspective from the viewing rock is one of earth-bound bodies giving rise to the spirit which sings with color and texture, dances along garden paths dreaming of flowers that are to be. Knowing that flexibility becomes artistry, Nature amends our plans, gracing us with opportunities. They are called elegance, beauty, and personal fulfillment.

Until one is committed,
there is hesitancy, the chance to draw back,
always ineffectiveness.

Concerning acts of initiative (and creation)
there is one elementary truth
the ignorance of which kills countless ideas
and splendid plans:

That the moment one definitely commits oneself
then Providence moves too.

All sorts of things occur to help one
that would never otherwise have occured.

A whole stream of events issues from the decision,
raising in one's favor all manner
of unforeseen incidents and meetings
and material assistance
which no man could have dreamt
would come his way

Whatever you can do, or dream you can, begin it.
Boldness has genius, power, and magic in it.

Begin it now.

——Goethe

Winter's frozen grasses cascade over
the retaining wall, creating their own
unique beauty.

*Life must, indeed, be motion, and motion sound; but let all the
sounds of human life bring harmony, and let them learn to make
their path melodious and sweet. Teach them to listen to the music
of the trees, show them the way firs and pines and beeches live,
swaying to the wind and singing all the time. They have swayed
and sung since Time was; now they are incapable, in any cir-
cumstances, of stridency or discord in their song.*

——Geoffrey Hodson

Hardie's Blossom Glossary

The beginning flower enthusiast, either gardener or arranger, is often intimidated by the vast number of flowers available at the florist's and in gardens. In an effort to speak to that feeling, I have pictured here my "favorite forty," which are rewarding growers or may be purchased from your florist. Generally speaking, flowers and materials featured in our seasonal designs, while esteemed, are not repeated in glossary photographs. This allows a wider range from which to make selections.

Cut flowers are imported by wholesalers from growers in the Caribbean Basin, Pacific Basin, France, Holland, Israel, and South Africa. They are produced domestically in greenhouses located in Arizona, California, Florida, and New Jersey. Differentiating between them can be confusing considering the profusion of sometimes unfamiliar varieties, many of which are found in flower shops "out-of-season."

Growing numerous varieties at home acquaints us with geographical adaptability, seasonal selections, and individual preferences. Some are charming as permanent garden residents. Others are cultivated to bring their vibrant energies indoors as cut flowers for the house.

Acer palmatum

Common name: Japanese Maple
Plant type: Deciduous tree
Hardiness zones: (5) 6–8
Interest: Leaves

The small, "fingered" foliage of Japanese maple adds depth of color to autumn flower designs. It conditions well and can be used in any size arrangement. Some varieties have green leaves that turn red in fall, while others have reddish colored leaves throughout the growing season which become brighter in fall. It is not available through flower shops.

Achillea spp.

Common name: Yarrow
Plant type: Perennial
Hardiness zones: 3–8 (9)
Interest: Flowers (early to late summer)

The large, colorful flowerheads and lacy foliage of yarrow make it a stunning addition to the garden and to fresh or dried arrangements. For arranging or drying, cut when the flowers are about half open. To dry quickly and easily, hang them upside down or allow them to dry in a container with a few inches of water in the bottom (don't let the flowerheads touch while drying). Yarrow is available through nurseries.

Alstroemeria

Common name: Peruvian lily
Plant type: Tender perennial
Hardiness zones: (6) 7–10
Interest: Flowers (spring to midsummer)

Alstroemeria requires cool, fertile, well-drained soil and can be somewhat temperamental, though once established, it spreads freely by roots and seeds. It needs winter protection in Zone 6. If you cannot grow it in your garden, it is available in flower shops year round. The colors include orange, yellow, pink to red, and lilac to white; often streaked and speckled with darker colors. The cut flowers are attractive in formal arrangements, and since they last about ten days, are an excellent investment.

Anemone hupehensis

Common name: Japanese anemone
Plant type: Perennial
Hardiness zones: 5–8
Interest: Flowers (late summer to fall)

Japanese anemone are fragile when cut and last longer if placed in water rather than in floral foam. Fill a glass vase to overbrimming with them. Not available from the florist, grow your own in a woodland-type soil with dappled shade. The pink, rose, or white, single blossoms are beautiful in the fall garden, where they combine well with caryopteris. Grow in woodland-type soil, in dappled shade. They are drought tolerant, and can be invasive.

Antirrhinhum majus

Common name: Snapdragon
Plant type: Tender perennial
Hardiness zones: 7–10
Interest: Flowers (early summer to fall)

Snapdragons overwinter easily in Virginia, if well mulched, but they are also often grown as annuals here and further north. They prefer rich soil, but are tolerant of drought conditions. Cut them back in July and feed with manure, to enjoy abundant late summer blooms. Available in a wide range of stunning colors, from white to yellow, orange, pink, red, mauve, and bicolored, their spikey shape adds interest and texture to arrangements. They last a week in water. Although readily available in flower shops, plan to order special colors ahead of time.

Begonia Semperflorans-Cultorum Hybrids

Common name: Wax begonia
Plant type: Tender perennial
Hardiness zone: 10
Interest: Flowers (spring to fall)

Housebound begonias, I call them, thrive in well-lighted indoor conditions, but they are also a very popular bedding plant in both sun and shade; they are not winter hardy. Single or double flowers in white to shades of pink or red blossom on long, brittle stems. Use as cut flowers in impromptu designs, placed formally or informally in small glass vases; they last exceedingly well. Purchase begonias from your greenhouse.

Callicarpa americana

Common name: Beautyberry
Plant type: Shrub
Hardiness zones: 7–10
Interest: Berries (late summer to fall)

Callicarpa has bluish flowers from late spring to early summer; in autumn it bears spectacular long, dense clusters of bright magenta-purple berries that accent any arrangement. It may be used fresh or dried. Easy to grow, it tolerates poor soils. It was planted in Thomas Jefferson's garden. I bought mine at the Monticello garden shop in Charlottesville, Viginia, which maintains a program for developing historic flowers and shrubs.

Caryopteris spp.

Common name: Bluebeard
Plant type: Shrub
Hardiness zones: 5–8 (9)
Interest: Flowers (late summer to early fall)

Caryopteris is one of the most beautiful fall bloomers, with its deep violet-blue flowers and slightly silver leaves. It prefers well-drained soil and a sunny location. Grown in masses as a background for chrysanthemums, it adds depth to flower beds. The two are attractive used together as cut flowers. You may purchase this rich blue flowering shrub at your nursery.

Celosia cristata

Common name: Cockscomb
Plant type: Annual
Interest: Flowers

Cockscomb prefers rich, evenly moist soil in a
sunny location. Reseeding freely, it is available
with either deep red to pink and yellow to peach
blossoms in the form of velvety caps. Although it
is readily available in late summer and early fall
from the florist, it is a satisfyingly productive
garden flower. Its several varieties bloom until
frost. Use freshly cut in late summer and fall, or
dried all year-round.

Dendranthema x grandiflorum

Common name: Florists' chrysanthemum
Plant type: Perennial
Hardiness zones: 5– 9
Interest: Flowers (late summer to fall)

Chrysanthemums, long a mainstay of late summer gardening, are easy to grow in well-drained
soil. Pinch back flower buds until early July to
promote heavier bloom from late summer until
frost. The sizes and varieties are remarkable,
ranging from small button mums to large-headed
'Fugis', cremones, spiders, and football mums. A
wide range of colors includes white to yellow,
orange, bronze, pink, and red to purple. Search
out unusual ones for the border. They have thick,
strongly aromatic leaves and are also available on
the market all year. Both in arrangements and in
the garden, they combine artfully with lilies and
autumn foliage.

Clematis spp.

Common name: Clematis
Plant type: Perennial vine
Hardiness zones: (3) 4–8
Interest: Flowers (spring to late summer, depending on species and variety)

Clematis is a woody vine that is in love with twine. To make it climb well, attach green garden twine to your trellis and watch the vines clamber up! It is easy to grow, drought tolerant, and undemanding of soil conditions. It bears large, single blossoms up to 5" in diameter. The dried seed cases are also useful. Clematis is of interest as cascading material in summer combinations; it must be "home-grown."

Coreopsis tripteris

Common name: Atlantic coreopsis
Plant type: Perennial
Hardiness zones: (3) 4–8
Interest: Flowers (summer to early fall)

Miniature black-eyed Susans form clumps and bloom incessantly. My parent plant grows four feet tall with many branching stems the entire summer. It is tolerant of a wide range of soil and moisture conditions, and does need full sun. Its yellow to yellow-orange blossoms with black seed-head centers add rich color to arrangements and are long-lasting as cut flowers. This 1" variety is not on the market.

Cosmos bipinnatus

Common name: Cosmos
Plant type: Annual
Interest: Flowers (summer to fall)

This variety of cosmos is willowy and tall, adding grace anywhere it is used, in the landscape or in casual summer designs for the house. With its single and double white, pink, or purple blossoms, 2"–4" in diameter, it works well as background, linear, or mass material. Easy to grow, it is very tolerant of a range of soils and also survives drought. It blooms prolifically from July until frost. Another species, *C. sulphureus,* has bright yellow, orange, or red blossoms. Both are available from the florist.

Dahlia

Common name: Dahlia
Plant type: Tender perennial
Hardiness zones: (8) 9–10
Interest: Flowers (summer to fall)

Dahlias are enormously responsive in the garden, a delight to grow and arrange. They are available in a wide range of heights, blossom sizes, and colors, including white, yellow, pink, red, purple, and bicolored. In the garden, they prefer sun and light loam. Large varieties need staking. When used in arrangements, they must be carefully conditioned and can look stiff; furthermore, purchased flowers are not long lasting. Arrange them in water, rather than in floral foam.

Daucus carota

Common name: Queen Anne's Lace
Plant type: Biennial
Hardiness zones: 3–10
Interest: Flowers (summer to early fall)

Queen Anne's lace is easy to grow and tolerates drought and poor soils, but it can be invasive. It prefers full sun, though it can be grown in some shade. Adoring to bloom, it has fragile-looking umbels of white with occasional tints of pale pink; at the center of the blossom is a distinctive small, black dot. In arrangements, it lasts beautifully in either water or floral foam, but consistently sheds on tabletops. Airy and cooling in summer's heat, you will find it everywhere!

Consolida ambigua

Common name: Larkspur
Plant type: Annual
Interest: Flowers (summer)

Sow larkspur seed generously in sun or light shade. It is very tolerant of soil and moisture ranges, and freely self-seeds. Prolific pink, blue, and white flowers will provide tall, spikey, colorful interest in garden corners. Massed casually in glass containers, this flower brings those corners indoors. Its tendriled side growth is nice in small vases, and its flowers and leaves add airiness to arrangements. Larkspur is available over a long season in flower shops and dries beautifully.

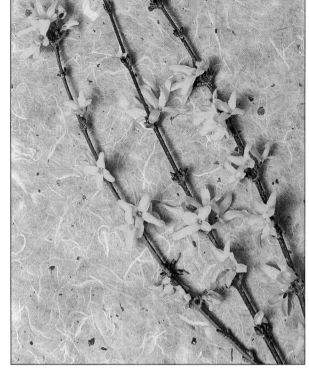

Euphorbia marginata

Common name: Snow-on-the-Mountain
Plant type: Annual
Interest: Leaves

A native American wildflower, striking, cool-looking snow-on-the-mountain is handsome grown with all summer annuals, and is one of my especially favorite "greens." It adds spirit wherever it is used and has a long lifetime in arrangements. Accepting a range of soil conditions and tolerating drought, it has variegated green-and-white upper leaves in late summer, surrounded by tiny white flowers. Use caution when cutting or arranging: the sap is a powerful skin irritant. Burn the cut ends to keep that milky substance from clouding the water in a glass vase. Snow-on-the-mountain is obtainable through florists.

Forsythia spp.

Common name: Forsythia
Plant type: Shrub
Hardiness zones: (4) 5–9
Interest: Flowers (spring)

Forsythia's branches are unsurpassed for use as linear material in arrangements any time of year, particularly in settings that require tall, dramatic designs. In spring, chrome yellow flowers bring instant cheer; in summer, leaves are a pleasing green; in fall and winter, the bark is rich brown with textured bud formations. Forsythia prefers full sun, accepting a wide range of soils and is drought-tolerant once established. Its arching, spreading branches root easily wherever they touch the ground. Cuttings also root readily. Kept under control by pruning, it adds spontaneity to the garden. Cut branches are available through flower shops, but the more interesting shapes are homegrown. Purchase plants at nurseries.

Heliotropium arborescens

Common name: Heliotrope
Plant type: Perennial
Hardiness zones: 9–10
Interest: Flowers (late spring to early fall)

A Victorian favorite, heliotrope enlivens garden beds or terra-cotta pots with its clusters of lilac-like purple-blue or white fragrant flowers and deep green foliage. It prefers rich, moist, well-drained soil, in a sunny or lightly shaded spot. Susceptible to frost, it may also be grown indoors. Purples do not show up well at night, so mix heliotrope with brights and whites to show it off in arrangements. I have never seen heliotrope for sale as a cut flower.

Hydrangea quercifolia

Common name: Oakleaf hydrangea
Plant type: Shrub
Hardiness zones: 5–9
Interest: Flowers (late spring to summer)

With its spreading shape, large, bold foliage, and showy white and cream clusters of pendulous blossoms, oakleaf hydrangea is gorgeous in the garden. It prefers moist shade or part sun and can withstand some drought conditions. As autumn approaches, the foliage becomes a brilliant red or purple, and the flowers fade to pale green and brown. To dry the blossoms for winter arrangements, cut long stems and place them in several inches of water in a tall bucket for support. Oakleaf and other hydrangeas are available from your florist.

Ilex x attenuata, Foster Hybrid Group

Common name: Foster's hybrid holly
Plant type: Shrub
Hardiness zones: 6–9
Interest: Leaves (evergreen); fruit (late summer through winter)

Foster holly has small, spinescent leaves that produce a color-enhancing effect on other winter evergreen foliage when they are placed together in gardens or in wreaths, garlands, or designs. They require a soil that is kept moist before it freezes and also need some protection from winter winds and sunshine. Both male and female shrubs are required if you want the fruits. In spring, the shrubs are covered with small, pale yellow flowers; brilliant red berries appear in fall and linger through winter, if not eaten by your birds. These shrubs are important additions to the landscape, especially in small gardens. Plants are available from garden centers.

Lavandula angustifolia

Common name: English lavender
Plant type: Perennial
Hardiness zones: 5–8 (9)
Interest: Leaves (evergreen); flowers (summer)

An old-fashioned herb with its deep blue and white spikes of tiny blossoms, lavender is very fragrant fresh or dried. It is drought resistant and accepts a variety of soil conditions. I like to cut 8" stems, tie them together in bundles, and place them between my linens. They are also luxurious added to the bath. Cut them longer to add to fresh bouquets for the summertime dinner table. The dried flowers continue to give off a pleasant aroma for years. Order them from catalogs.

Leucodendron

Common name:
Plant type: Shrub or small tree
Hardiness zones: 10
Interest: Flowers

Silver tree's male flowerheads have colorful "tips" that make a nice play with chrysanthemums and other fall flowers. Leathery leaves surround both the terminal sessile male flowers and the female conelike heads. This "green" can also be used alone with drama. It is long lasting and dries well. Although it can usually be found in flower shops, it's a good idea to call ahead if you wish to special order it.

'Rainbow'
ng leucthoe

Hardiness zones: (4) 5–8
Interest: Leaves (evergreen); flowers (spring)

Leucothoe can best be described as "trailing material." Its variegated leaves bring liveliness to gardens and arrangements. Low-growing, gracefully arching branches are covered with dark, deep green foliage that turns bronze with purple tints in winter. In late April and May, tiny bell-shaped flowers appear at the tips of branches. It prefers rich, acid soil and partial shade. Use this pliant, obedient plant lavishly in arrangements. It must be homegrown.

Lilium Hybrids

Common name: Lily
Plant type: Perennial
Hardiness zones: 4–8
Interest: Flowers (summer)

Dramatic, upright sprays of large blossoms in colors ranging from white, yellow, and orange to pink, red, purple, and bicolored, make hybrid lilies a favorite during all seasons. In addition, their longevity as cut flowers is exceptional. Plant in partial shade and well-drained soil. Hybrid Asiatics (36"–48" with upward-facing blossoms), Orientals (30"–48" with outward-facing blossoms, and Trumpets (32" with outward-facing or drooping blossoms) bloom in the garden from June to September, but they are readily available on the market and their broad range of colors makes them useful during all seasons. Note: Lilies cut from the garden might not bloom the following year. Be careful of the pollen, which stains clothing and table linens.

Lysimachia clethroides

Common name: Gooseneck loosestrife
Plant type: Perennial
Hardiness zones: 3–8
Interest: Flowers (midsummer to late summer)

Gooseneck loosestrife's white arching sprays with tiny, white, bell-shaped flowers are attention-getters in late summer flower combinations. The stems are graceful used in "bulk" or with heliotrope. Their autumn foliage is also attractive. They grow easily in moist, rich soil and full sun. Because they can be invasive, you may wish to isolate them. They may be ordered from your florist.

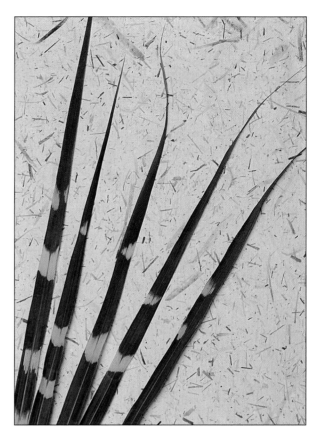

Matthiola incana

Common name: Stock
Plant type: Annual
Interest: Flowers (early summer to fall)

Stock's branching growth habit produces magnificent multiple flower spikes with blossom colors ranging from lilac, purple, maroon, and red, to yellow and white. With their sweet, spicy-clove scent, they are a marvelous addition to a fragrance garden. Plant in full sun and well-drained soil. Available at florists all year long, stock adds winter opulence to flower arrangements. Its fragrance and color range can wake up a room, while attractively shaped spikes give visual weight when inserted deeply into your design. Experiment by using masses of them together in a glass vase. Before conditioning, take time to peel their lower stems (as you would broccoli) and you'll find they last longer.

Miscanthus sinensis 'Zeberinus'

Common name: Zebra grass
Plant type: Perennial
Hardiness zones: 4–9
Interest: Leaves (spring to fall); fruit (fall to winter)

Zebra grass is a tall, imposing, ornamental grass, useful in dramatic groupings, fresh or dried. It has bold horizontal stripes and tassel-like fruit that appears late in the season, adding elegance to a winter landscape. Easy to grow, it tolerates a range of soil and moisture conditions. Ask a friend for a start of this fast-growing beauty.

G
L
O
S
S
A
R
Y

Nandina

Common name: Heavenly bamboo
Plant type: Shrub
Hardiness zones: (6) 7–9
Interest: Berries and foliage (fall)

The handsome, deep red foliage growing on long canes, topped by clusters of bright red berries adds radiance to tall arrangements from Thanksgiving through the entire winter. Earlier in the fall, the rosy-green berries enhance "all-green" foliage combinations. Heavenly bamboo is easy to establish in sun or shade. It likes moisture. Plants are readily available at nurseries.

Pelargonium x hortorum

Common name: Zonal geranium
Plant type: Tender perennial
Hardiness zones: 10
Interest: Flowers (spring to fall)

Commonly grown as container or bedding plants, zonal geraniums also add informal, colorful interest in designs. Available in many shades of white, pink, and red, as well as bicolored, they work well with veronica and roses or ferns. Dig plants before winter, wash off the roots, and hang plants upside down in a garage or basement. Repot in spring or early summer and water thoroughly. Other species include many scented cultivars, useful dried as sachets or in herbal bouquets to hang in closets. All kinds are readily available at local greenhouses.

Photinia glabra

Common name: Japanese photinia
Plant type: Shrub
Hardiness zones: 7–9
Interest: Leaves (evergreen)

An important hedge and foundation plant in warmer regions of North America, *Photinia glabra* can be espaliered easily, and its red tips (from which it gets its common name) are attractive in the landscape. The glabrous leaves are red when young. Red tips work well as filler for arrangements any time of year. Plants are available at nurseries.

Pieris japonica

Common name: Japanese pieris
Plant type: Shrub
Hardiness zones: 2–7 (8)
Interest: Leaves (evergreen); flowers (spring)

Pieris has graceful, spreading foliage that form clusters of somewhat glossy leaves. Unlike many evergreens, its coloring enhances flowers, rather than drinking up their colors. A year-round winner, it has white, bell-shaped flowers that bloom in spring; seed capsules that are picturesque in autumn; flower buds that hang in tassels in winter. Pieris is available at nurseries. Plant in neutral to acid soil, in sun to partial shade.

Platycodon grandiflorus

Common name: Balloonflower
Plant type: Perennial
Hardiness zones: 3–8
Interest: Flower (early to midsummer)

You will meet pink and white balloonflowers, but
the exquisite blue variety draws special attention
to flower borders as well as to impromptu
arrangements. To help cut flowers last, burn their
stem ends before placing them in water. Do not
use floral foam. Plants 24"–30" tall are easy to
grow from seed. Position in well-drained garden
loam, in sun to light shade. Flowers are available
at flower shops in the summer.

Physostegia virginiana

Common name: Obedience
Plant type: Perennial
Hardiness zones: 2–9
Interest: Flowers (late summer to early fall)

Lavender- and pink-flowered physostegia out-
grows everything in the fall garden and is
delightful in combination with goldenrod in or
out of vases. White-flowered physostegia brings
end-of-summer interest as companion to
anemones. Its stems are square with hinged
joints, making it easy to bend blossoms in any
direction you wish. Planted in light, moist soil
and a shady location, physostegia will form erect
clumps. Order cut flowers through your florist,
buy plants from the nursery, or plant seeds.

Rudbeckia hirta

Common name: Gloriosa daisy
Plant type: Perennial
Hardiness zones: 3–9
Interest: Flowers (mid to late summer)

The eye-catching colorations (yellow to orange and bicolored) of sizable gloriosa daisy flower heads brighten the summer border. Attractive planted with their cousins, black-eyed Susans, they are easy to grow, tolerant of a range of soil and moisture conditions, prefer sun but can take partial shade. They grow to 18"–24", forming clumps. A favorite of goldfinches, the black seed heads are attractive when dry. Splendid in short-lived arrangements, gloriosa daisies prefer to be gathered in the cool of the evening. Place them immediately in vases filled with warm water (skipping the conditioning stage) to enjoy on the dinner table. Seeds are found in gardening catalogs and seedlings can be bought at greenhouses.

Spirea spp.

Common name: Spirea
Plant type: Shrub
Hardiness zones: 3–9
Interest: Flowers (spring to mid summer)

That old-fashioned treasure, bridal wreath, adds grace wherever it goes. It serves effectively as a background garden shrub, screening out the unsightly. Umbel clusters of tiny white flowers grow close to the branch on short stems in late spring. Easy to grow in sun or light shade, this 5– to 6–foot shrub tolerates most soil conditions. Spirea's branches, whether in bloom or not, work as both filler and line material in design work. There are also summer-blooming spireas, with flat-topped clusters of tiny flowers borne at the tips of branches. Look for white *albiflora* and pink to purple-red *S. x bumalda* 'Anthony Waterer'. Purchase spireas at your garden center.

Syringa vulgaris

Common name: Lilac
Plant type: Shrub
Hardiness zones: 3–7 (8)
Interest: Flowers (spring)

Upright lilacs have straight, heavy branches and stems, and heart-shaped leaves. The very fragrant deep to light purple and white flowers grow on panicles up to 8" long, with ½" florets. Twelve to 20' tall, shrubs are very hardy and long-lived. They prefer slightly alkaline or neutral, fertile, moist soil, but tolerate some drought. Order from the florist as early as the beginning of December. Try this experiment: Cut lilac branches in January; they will leaf out in ten days' time indoors, given plenty of light, in a vase filled with water. "Miniature" blooms (usually white, even from a shrub that habitually produces lavender flower heads) will follow, if you are lucky — complete with fragrance. The leaves usually wilt as blossoms appear, but can be pinched off if unsightly.

Tulipa spp.

Common name: Tulip
Plant type: Perennial
Hardiness zones: 3–8
Interest: Flowers (mid to late spring)

Tulips come in a wide variety, including very early-blooming Kaufmanniana and Greigii, mid-season Triumph and Darwin Hybrids, and late spring-flowering Darwins, lily-flowered, Parrots, and Cottage tulips. Ranging from 4"–20" tall, tulips bear 2"–3", cup-shaped, six-petaled flowers, in most colors except blue. Plant in the garden in deep, fertile, well-drained soil, or in containers. You can grow a wider range of sizes with more intense colorations than you'll find in commercially available cut tulips. Available on the market from late November until late spring, a bunch of French tulips is a real treat in January! Either massed in vases or used as line material, tulips lend an air of sprightliness.

Viola x wittrockiana

Common name: Pansy
Plant type: Annual
Interest: Flowers (spring and fall)

Pansies add spontaneity to the garden, with their 2"–3" single blooms in many combinations of white, yellow, purple, blue, and maroon. Growing 4"–8" tall, they make a fine edging for spring-blooming perennials. They prefer soil enriched with manure, and will bloom continually if the dead flowers are consistently removed. Use in small bouquets placed in water (the stems are too fragile for floral foam), or grow in small pots which can come inside for the dining table. Buy plants from your garden center in spring or fall (in warmer regions).

Zinnia elegans

Common name: Zinnia
Plant type: Annual
Interest: Flowers (summer to fall)

The brilliance of summer is reflected in all the zinnia colors — white, yellow, chartreuse, orange, red, and purple. Zinnias love heat and sun and tolerate poor soil and drought. Tall varieties (zinnias are available in heights from 1'–4') combine beautifully with themselves. I always grow both the chartreuse and white ones to mix with "vivids"! Buy them from the florist if you don't wish to grow them.

Flower color list

The following suggestions, flowers categorized by color, may be found in seed catalogues, at nurseries (purchased as seedlings in flats), or may be ordered through your flower shops.

Yellow Family

Alstroemeria
Black-eyed Susan
Chrysanthemum
Columbine
Coreopsis
Cushion spurge
Dahlia
Daisy
Eremurus
Euphorbia fulgens
Forsythia
Gaillardia
Gerbera
Gladiolus
Goldenrod
Iris
Jonquil
Lady's mantle
Lily
Marigold
Narcissus
Pansy
Rose
Snapdragon
Sunflower
Tulip
Yarrow

White Family

Acidanthera
Alstroemeria
Amaryllis
Aster
Astilbe
Baby's breath
Begonia
Bleeding heart
Buddleia
Carnation
Chrysanthemum
Clematis
Cleome
Columbine
Cosmos
Cyclamen
Dahlia
Daisy
Echinacea
Euphorbia fulgens
Feverfew
Gardenia
Geranium
Gerbera
Hyacinth
Iris
Larkspur
Lilac
Lily

Lily of the valley
Lisianthus
Lisimachia
Money plant, dried
Narcissus
Nicotiana
Pansy
Peony
Petunia
Phlox
Physostegia
Poinsettia
Queen Anne's lace
Rose
Salvia
Snapdragon
Spirea
Stock
Sweet pea
Tulip
Veronica
Viburnum
Wax flower
Yarrow

Pink Family

Alstroemeria
Aster
Astilbe
Azalea
Bee balm
Begonia
Bleeding heart
Columbine
Coral bells
Cosmos
Dahlia
Delphinium
Dianthus
Geranium
Gerbera
Gladiolus
Hyacinth
Iris
Ixia,
Larkspur
Lilac
Lily
Lisianthus
Mountain laurel
Nerine
Nicotiana
Pansy
Peony
Petunia
Phlox
Poinsettia
Rhododendron
Sedum

Snapdragon
Spirea 'Anthony Waterer'
Sweet pea
Tulip
Weigela
Zinnia

Red Family

Alstroemeria
Amaryllis
Anthurium
Columbine
Euphorbia fulgens
Geranium
Iris
Lily
Petunia
Poinsettia
Pyracantha, berries
Rose
Salvia splendens
Sedum
Tulip
Zinnia

Purple Family

Allium gigantium
Aster
Azalea
Bee balm
Bell flower
Buddleia
Clematis
Columbine
Cosmos
Cyclamen
Dahlia
Delphinium
Dianthus
Echinacea
Geranium
Gerbera
Gladiolus
Globe thistle
Heather
Iris
Joe Pye weed
Larkspur
Lavender
Liatris
Lilac
Lisianthus
Loosestrife
Money plant
Nicotiana
Pansy
Peony
Petunia
Phlox

Physostegia
Rhododendron
Rose
Salvia superba and
    splendens
Scabiosa
Sea lavender
Snapdragon
Stock
Sweet pea
Tulip
Wax flower
Yarrow
Zinnia

Orange Family

Alstroemeria
Amaryllis
Anthurium
Azalea
Bird of Paradise
Cosmos
Crab apple
Crocosmia
Dahlia
Euphorbia fulgens
Geranium
Gladiolus
Kalanchoe
Lily
Marigold
Nasturtium
Pyracantha
Rose
Tulip
Zinnia

Blue Family

Agapanthus
Ageratum
Aster
Blue bells
Buddleia
Caryopteris
Clematis
Columbine
Delphinium
Grape hyacinth
Hyacinth
Iris
Larkspur
Nigella
Rose
Russian sage
Salvia officinalis
Scabiosa
Veronica

House Plants

House plants can be both beautiful and useful. However, quite a few of them can cause severe discomfort or illness, and contact should be avoided. This isn't to say that you shouldn't continue to enjoy house plants. However, you should be careful to keep them out of reach of pets and children. The following are plants that are known to be hazardous:

Azalea
Cactii
Caladium
Century plant
Chrysanthemum
Dieffenbachia
Elephant ear
English ivy
Eucalyptus
Four o'clocks
Heliotrope
Hydrangea
Iris
Oleander
Peperomia
Petunia
Philodendron
Poinsettia
Prayer plant
Primrose
Rex begonia
Rubber plant
Sago palm

Acknowledgments

Behind an endeavor of this scope, a community of creators is at work—singly producing a unique facet of the whole. Each knows what he or she has given, each has contributed grandly. Their loyalty enriches me.

Special Mentors (in alphabetical order):
Charlotte Abel, John Casey, David Davis, Beverly Galbreath, Douglas C. Larsen, Robert R. Leichtman, M.D., Terry A. Smith, Helen Yamada, and my family

Special thanks . . .
To Amy Hammond, editor, who devoted initiative and talent to making my handwritten copy into a polished manuscript; Kathy Klingaman, award-winning designer; Sunny Reynolds, exceptional photographer; Rue Judd, botanical wizard; my adroit agent, Kathleen Hughes, who wore many hats, transforming the efforts of our resourceful team into final book form; and Kate Hartson, our editor at Park Lane Press, whose encouragement and insight brought this latest dream to life.

To Peg Mailler, Martha N. Law, and Gayle Bathon, steadfast loyalists; Mimi Lee, accomplished rosarian; Penne Poole, up-to-the-minute designer; Robin Turner, who graciously gave her time.

Plants People:
Charlene Breeden, Etlan, Virginia
Mason H. Hutcheson, Culpeper, Virginia
Piedmont Growers, Bealeton, Virginia
Willow Run Company, Elkwood, Virginia

Those who furnished their wares, wits, and talents for the photographs:
Dawn Barusky, Village Flowers, Warrenton, Virginia
Chez Fox Antiques, Keswick, Virginia
Dulaney Hollow Antiques, Madison, Virginia
Andrew Haley and the staff of Airlie Center, Warrenton, Virginia
Craig Hartman, Chef, Clifton Country Inn, Charlottesville, Virginia
Sharon Peterson, Kester Wholesale Floral Comp.
Red Barn Antiques, Criglersville, Virginia
Jane Jenkins, All in a Row, Warrenton, Virginia
Pat Roberts, Hebron Valley Florist, Madison, Virginia
Roxanne Weeks, Pennock Co., Springfield, Virginia

Credits

Picnic, page 83
Credits: Quilt and wooden bowls from Red Barn Antiques, Criglersville, Virginia. Ice-cream freezer and baskets from Dulaney Hollow Antiques, Madison, Virginia. Food designed by Clifton Inn Bed and Breakfast, Charlottesville, Virginia.

Childrens Tea Party, pages 97-99
Credits: teacups and appointments from Chez Fox Antiques, Keswick, Virginia. Benches from Red Barn Antiques, Criglersville, Virginia. Chairs, dolls, and doll's high chair from Dulaney Hollow Antiques, Madison, Virginia. Food designed by Clifton Inn.

Silver Winter Arrangement
Credit: Fabric, layout, and table design by Penne Poole Interior Designs of Washington, D.C.

Quote, page 71
From Gabriele Uhlen, *Meditations with Hildegard of Bingen* (Santa Fe: Bear & Co., Inc., 1983), p. 24.

Quote, page 104
Translation of Rudolf Steiner's "Tischebet" or "Grace." Steiner's works are available in English from Anthroposophic Press, Inc., Hudson, New York 12534.

Quote, page 130
From Lawrence Kushner, *Honey from the Rock*, (Woodstock, Vermont: Jewish Lights Publishing, 1977), p. 89-90. Book available ($14.95 + $3.50 s/h) and permission granted by Jewish Lights Publishing, P.O. Box 237, Woodstock, Vermont 05091.

Recipe for Quenched Wine, page 146
From Dr. Wighard Stehlow and Gottfried Hertzka, M.D., *Hildegard of Bingen's Medicine* (Santa Fe, N.M.: Bear & Co., Inc., 1988), p. 86.

Quote, page 163
From Geoffrey Hodson, *Brotherhood of Angels & Men* (Wheaton, Illinois: Theosophical Publishing House, 1988), p. 41.

Subject Index

Page references in *italic* indicate illustrations.

Plant Index

The U.S.D.A. Plant Hardiness Zone Map

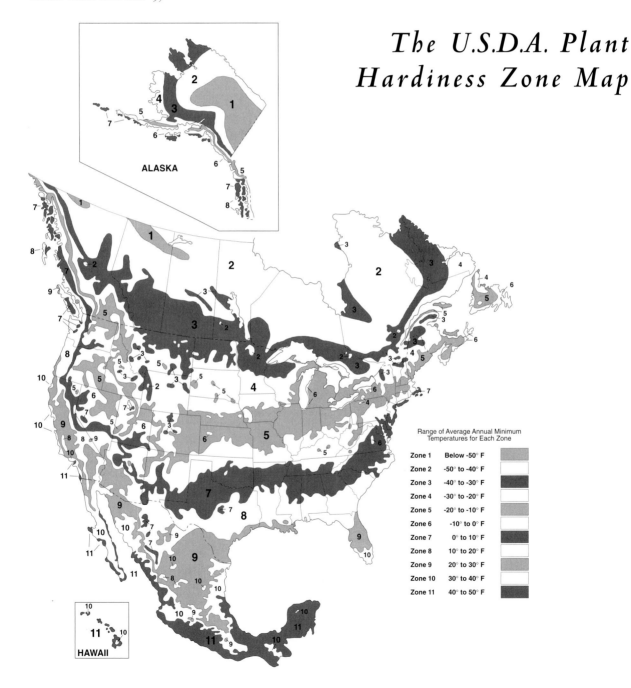

ALASKA

HAWAII

Range of Average Annual Minimum
Temperatures for Each Zone

Zone 1	Below -50° F
Zone 2	-50° to -40° F
Zone 3	-40° to -30° F
Zone 4	-30° to -20° F
Zone 5	-20° to -10° F
Zone 6	-10° to 0° F
Zone 7	0° to 10° F
Zone 8	10° to 20° F
Zone 9	20° to 30° F
Zone 10	30° to 40° F
Zone 11	40° to 50° F